BRON

To martin
may all your paths lead
in the right direction!
love marje wilson.

A CROSS-COUNTRY FOOTPATH
WITH CIRCULAR WALKS

by

Marje Wilson

for the Ramblers' Association
(West Riding Area)

The Ramblers

Other publications by the Ramblers' Association (West Riding Area)

Dales Way Handbook (with the Dales Way Association, annually)
Kiddiwalks (new edition Spring 1995)
Douglas Cossar, Ramblers' Leeds (1995)
Douglas Cossar, The Airedale Way (1996)
Douglas Cossar, Ramblers' Wakefield (1997)

The Brontë Way first published 1997

© Marje Wilson 1997

RAMBLERS' ASSOCIATION (WEST RIDING AREA)
27 Cookridge Avenue, Leeds LS16 7NA

ISBN 1 901184 05 6

Cover illustrations
Front: Oakwell Hall and Gawthorpe Hall;
Back: Ponden Hall (all by Fred Payne)

Publishers' Note
At the time of publication all footpaths used in these walks were
designated as public rights of way or permissive footpaths, or were paths
over which access has traditionally not been denied, but it should be
borne in mind that diversion orders may be made or permissions
removed. Although every care has been taken in the preparation of this
guide, neither the author nor the publisher can accept responsibility for
those who stray from the routes described.

Contents

The Country Code
- Enjoy the countryside and respect its life and work.
- Guard against all risk of fire
- Leave all gates as you find them: closed, if they are closed, open, if they are open.
- Keep your dogs under close control.
- Keep to public paths across farmland.
- Use gates and stiles to cross fences, hedges and walls.
- Leave livestock, crops and machinery alone.
- Take your litter home.
- Do not pollute any water.
- Protect wildlife, plants and trees.
- Take special care on country roads.
- Make no unnecessary noise.

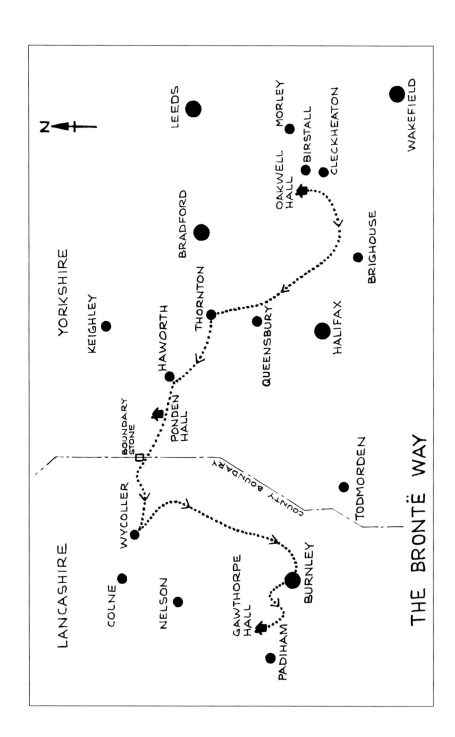

THE BRONTË WAY

THE BRONTË WAY
Introduction

The Brontë Way is a long distance footpath of some 69 kilometres/43 miles from Oakwell Hall, Birstall, near Leeds in West Yorkshire to Gawthorpe Hall, Padiham, in Lancashire. It links together a variety of places which played a part in the lives and literary productions of the Brontë family, embracing paths which must have been used by the Reverend Patrick Brontë as he went about his ministry and others used by his daughters when they were visiting friends or taking walks in the countryside which inspired their novels. It also offers an attractive introduction to the pastoral and moorland landscapes of the South Pennines.

The Brontë Way shares part of its route with the following other long-distance paths: the Kirklees Way, the Calderdale Way, the Worth Way, the Pennine Way, the Pendle Way and the Burnley Way.

Hitherto the only guide to the Brontë Way has been a series of four leaflets produced by the Standing Conference of South Pennine Authorities (SCOSPA). Excellent though these are, with a wealth of historical information, colour photographs, drawings, maps and a route description, they do have drawbacks, not the least of which are that the route description is rather sketchy in places, the maps are artist's impressions which are of little use for route-finding and the two Yorkshire leaflets describe the route from east to west, the two Lancashire ones from west to east! A revised version of the leaflets is being published in the autumn of 1997 and will be available in local TICs.

The present guide book has been written primarily with the practical needs of walkers in mind, to provide a detailed description of the route of the path and just a few historical and literary notes on the places visited.

I have tried to cater for three distinct types of walker. There will be those who see the Brontë Way primarily as a linear route, and they will want to start at one end and walk straight through to the other, either without stopping, or by breaking their journey at hotels or bed and breakfast establishments on the way. For them I have provided information at the end of the book on finding suitable accommodation.

The second type are those who again see the Way as a linear walk, but who divide it up into sections and make each section into a day's walk, using public transport to reach the starting points of each section and to take them home again at the end. The number of sections and the length of each section will be a matter of personal preference, determined partly by the availability of public transport. The following scheme has been proved practicable by many walkers.

The route is divided up into four sections, giving four day walks.

Day 1   Oakwell Hall to Shelf (10¼ miles, 16½ km). At the start take the 251/252 Bradford-Dewsbury bus from Bradford Interchange to the stop on the Dewsbury Road (A652) nearest to the access road to Oakwell Hall Country Park and walk up this to the Hall. At the end take the 571 Halifax-Bradford or the 570 Sowerby Bridge-Bradford bus from Shelf Hall Park back into Bradford.

Day 2   Shelf to Haworth (10¾ miles, 17½ km). At the start take the 571 Bradford-Halifax or the 570 Bradford-Sowerby Bridge bus from Bradford Interchange to Shelf Hall Park. At the end take the 663/664/665/698/699 bus from Haworth to Bradford.

Day 3   Haworth to Wycoller (7½ miles, 12 km, with an additional 1¼ miles, 2 km at the end from Wycoller to Laneshaw Bridge). At the start take either the train from Bradford to Keighley and the Keighley and Worth Valley train from Keighley to Haworth or the 663/664/665 Bradford-Keighley-Haworth bus to Haworth. At the end walk from Wycoller to Laneshaw Bridge and take the 22/24/25 bus to Keighley.

Day 4   Wycoller to Gawthorpe Hall (14¼ miles, 22¾ km, with an additional 1¼ miles, 2 km at the start from Laneshaw Bridge to Wycoller). At the start take the 22/24/25 Keighley-Burnley bus to Laneshaw Bridge and walk to Wycoller, using the route of Day 3 in reverse. At the end there is a frequent bus service along the main road by Gawthorpe Hall into Burnley and transfer to the 22/24/25 Burnley-Keighley bus.

The third type of walker are those who prefer a gentler sort of walking in the form of circular rambles, the start of which can be reached if possible either by public transport or by car. For them I have divided the route up into eleven sections and made each section into a circular walk, so that the Brontë Way can be collected bit by bit perhaps over a series of winter weekends.

The route of the Brontë Way can be located on the Ordnance Survey Landranger maps 104 (Leeds, Bradford & Harrogate) and 103 (Blackburn and Burnley). At a scale of 1:25 000 you would need Pathfinder sheets 692 (Dewsbury), 691 (Halifax), 682 (Bradford) and the Outdoor Leisure map 21 (South Pennines). At the start of each walk I have indicated which of these maps are necessary for it. The sketch maps which accompany the route descriptions are based on the O.S. Pathfinder maps and are reproduced with the permission of the Controller of Her Majesty's Stationery Office © Crown copyright 43323U. They are intended to give an overview of the walks and to supplement the description, but as they are greatly simplified, particularly in built-up areas, **they should not be used as a substitute for the description.**

Where the walks are accessible by public transport, I have given details as they are known to me at the moment. But please do check this information before you set out. Within the West Yorkshire area, bus and train information can be obtained from Metroline (0113-245-7676), in Lancashire buses are provided by Keighley & District Travel (01535-611606) or Burnley & Pendle Transport (01282-425245).

The following Tourist Information Centres may also be sources of useful information:

Bradford (01274-753678); Halifax (01422-368725); Huddersfield (01484-430808); Haworth (01535-642329); Nelson (01282-692890); Burnley (01282-55485).

Route directions for the Brontë Way are printed in **bold** in the text, return routes are in ordinary type, matters of interest are printed in *italic*.

I hope that you will not meet with any problems on the way, but if you do, please report them to the appropriate local authority. These are:

Public Rights of Way Unit, Kirklees MBC, Highways Service, Flint Street, Fartown, Huddersfield HD1 6LG (01484-225575).

Countryside Services, Calderdale Leisure Services, Wellesley Park, Halifax HX2 0AY (01422-359454).

Rights of Way Section, Bradford MDC, Holycroft, Goulbourne Street, Keighley BD21 1PY (01535-618300).

Countryside Access Officer, Pendle Borough Council, Highways & Transportation, Booth Street, Nelson BB9 7PX (01282-661661).

Countryside Access Officer, Burnley Borough Council, PO Box 29, Parker Lane Offices, Burnley BB11 2DT (01282-425011 Ext. 2544).

Happy wayfaring through Brontëland.

Marje Wilson
October 1997

Acknowledgments

I am indebted to the following people, without whose valuable support this book would not have been written. Donald Moore for reviewing the route. Fred Payne for the illustrations. Mike Smith for the overview map of the whole route. The Cathedral Centre, Bradford for providing survey companions. Douglas Cossar has edited the manuscript, provided the descriptions of the circular walks and drawn the route maps.

The following are the approximate distances in kilometres/miles from the start of the Way:

Clough House (A649)	6 kilometres/3¾ miles.
Bailiff Bridge (A58)	12 kilometres/7½ miles.
Shelf A6036	16½ kilometres/10¼ miles.
Clayton Heights A647	19½ kilometres/12 miles.
Thornton B6145	22½ kilometres/14 miles.
Denholme A629	26 kilometres/16 miles.
Haworth centre	34 kilometres/21 miles.
Wycoller village	46 kilometres/28½ miles.
Swinden Bridge	56 kilometres/34¾ miles.
Heasandford A6114	60 kilometres/37¼ miles.
New in Pendle Bridge	63½ kilometres/39½ miles.
Gawthorpe Road A671	68 kilometres/42¼ miles.
Gawthorpe Hall	68¾ kilometres/42¾ miles.

The Ramblers' Association

*What do **we** do?*

- We work non-stop to protect footpaths.
- We campaign for more freedom of access to mountain, moorland, woodland and other open country.
- We defend the beauty and diversity of Britain's countryside.

Sixty years of successful lobbying at local and national level have been entirely dependent on membership subscriptions, donations and legacies.

We are a registered charity with over 120,000 members working hard to promote the health and educational benefits of walking in the countryside.

The **West Riding Area** is one of the 51 Areas of the Ramblers' Association which cover England, Wales and Scotland. It includes the whole of West Yorkshire and parts of North Yorkshire around Selby, York, Harrogate, Ripon, Skipton and Settle, as well as the southern part of the Yorkshire Dales National Park. The Area has over 4.000 members and is divided into 13 Local Groups.

*What can **you** do?*

If you use and enjoy the footpath network, please remember what the Ramblers' Association has done to make this possible and help us to protect it, by becoming a member now. For further information write either to

Mrs Dora Tattersall, West Riding Area Membership Secretary,
10 Woodvale Grove, Lidget Green, Bradford BD7 2SL
or The Ramblers' Association, 1/5 Wandsworth Road, London SW8 2XX.

Oakwell Hall to Hartshead Church
Walk 1

Length of circular walk: 10 miles (16¼ km). *Length of Brontë Way* 4¾ miles (7½ km). A feast of Brontë associations on this first section, with fine views over the Spen valley. The return route to Oakwell Hall is very pleasant, almost entirely rural, through varied countryside, on good paths and tracks.

Maps: Pathfinder 692 and 691.

Start and finish: Oakwell Hall, Birstall. Park in the car park near the Hall, Information Centre and café. Oakwell Hall Country Park is open throughout the year from dawn until dusk. The Hall is open throughout the year Monday to Friday 11.00-17.00, Saturday and Sunday 12.00-17.00. There is a small seasonal admission charge to the Hall. Refreshments are served at the Oak Tree Café at the side of the Hall, which is open on weekdays from 11-5 and at weekends from 12-5.

By bus: Take the 251/252 Bradford-Dewsbury bus from Bradford Interchange to the stop on the Dewsbury Road (A652) nearest to the access road to Oakwell Hall Country Park and walk up this to the Hall.

'SHIRLEY COUNTRY'

Oakwell Hall, an Elizabethan manor house, was built by the Batt family and is today furnished as it might have been around 1690. It is depicted as 'Fieldhead', the home of Shirley Keelder in Charlotte Brontë's novel 'Shirley' which was published in 1849. The great hall within the building is described in detail by Charlotte who visited here frequently with her school friend Ellen Nussey. It was at that time a girls' school.

From the front door of Oakwell Hall turn left to pass between the gateposts and bear right down the drive, passing through the main gates onto a tarmac lane.Turn left and immediately right down an unsurfaced track, as indicated by a blue arrow on a wooden sign displaying two walkers which says 'Walk this way'. Walk down the field, cross a stream by a stone bridge and pass a lilac tree on the right which in the appropriate season has delightfully scented mauve blossoms, to reach the main A652 road. The Brontë Way crosses straight over to follow Monk Ings opposite.

A short detour, not part of the Way, may be made here by turning left along the main road, crossing it with care at Cambridge Road and taking the footpath opposite. Cross a wooden bridge, climb the bank and bear left round the lake. At the end of the lake turn left and cross the road into the churchyard of St. Peter's Parish Church, Birstall. The first tomb on the left is Ellen Nussey's and the inscription to her is on the far side.

St. Peter's Parish Church, Birstall, was the model for 'Briarfield Church' in the book 'Shirley'. The home of Ellen Nussey and her family was 'The Rydings', a fine old house built in its own grounds not far away. Charlotte Brontë was always welcomed here and she portrayed it as 'Thornfield Hall' in her novel 'Jane Eyre'. The Black Bull Inn to the west of the church was the Court Room where proceedings were held for petty theft offences.

OAKWELL HALL
('Fieldhead')

Retrace your steps along the Bradford Road to turn left into Monk Ings. **After about 100 metres take an unmade track forking left, between the houses. The Way from here is indicated with Brontë Way waymarks - usually a yellow arrow on a pink background. A waymark on a wooden post to the left of a modern bungalow points through a narrow stile. Walk straight up the middle of the field, pass through a cross hedge by a single stone gatepost and keep forward to the next field boundary, where there is a stile by another single stone post. Continue forward up the next field, bearing slightly right to a line of concrete fencing posts, and keep to the right of these to go through what used to be a kissing gate. Ignore the overgrown path ahead between low stone walls and pass into the field on the right. Follow the field edge with the wall/hedge on your left, then leave the field and follow a wall on your right, soon** entering the next field, where you bear left up a track. When you reach a modern housing estate, follow the tarmac road between the houses, bearing right and then left to reach the A651. Cross the road and turn left to arrive at the Red House Museum.

The Red House is so named because it is built in red brick, thus differing from the stone properties which are more typical of the area. It was built in 1660 by William Taylor, whose family owned it until 1920. Charlotte Brontë often visited Mary Taylor, who became one of her closest friends. She encouraged Charlotte to go to Brussels, which provided her with experiences used in her novels 'Villette' and 'The Professor'. They met at Miss Wooler's school, Roe Head, Mirfield. The Taylor family of Red House featured as the Yorkes of Briarmains in Charlotte's novel 'Shirley'.

Enter the Red House car park and walk up the grass to the top. Pass through a gap in the wall in front of a large factory and turn left along the narrow snicket *(local dialect for a narrow path between buildings or walls; in some parts of Yorkshire 'ginnel' is used)* to the main A643 road. Cross with care, turn right and walk a little way along the pavement to a gateway into the churchyard of St. Mary's Church, Gomersal. Follow the tarmac path to the left round the church and leave the churchyard again by the west gate. *(Just before you pass through the gate, turn right for 20 metres to the upright headstone which marks Mary Taylor's grave.)*

Turn left along Shirley Road *(the 'Shirley' estate is named after Charlotte's novel)*, keeping straight forward at the roundabout. The road narrows to a pleasant lane 'twixt high wall and well-kept gardens. Follow it to the end and cross Upper Lane to a gap in the wall opposite, then continue down the right hand edge of the field to a stile at the bottom - a Brontë Way waymark points right along Lower Lane. Pass No.52 Sisters' Houses.

No.52 Sisters' Houses was the home of Miss Margaret Wooler and her sisters before they set up school at Roe Head, Mirfield. Margaret Wooler gave Charlotte away on her marriage to Reverend Arthur Bell Nicholls.

Immediately after the bend, to the right of the drive of house no. 33, take the signposted footpath on the left. Follow the garden fence round to two stiles, one ahead, one on the right. Cross the one on the right and continue along the top of the field. There are panoramic views of the Spen Valley with Emley Moor television mast in the background. Cross a wooden stile into a field and bear very slightly left across it, passing to the left of a hedge corner, to the next stile in the far left hand corner. Cross it, go straight over

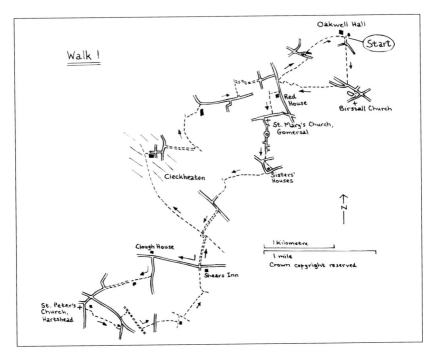

Walk I

Oakwell Hall

Start

Birstall Church

Red House

St. Mary's Church, Gomersal

Sisters' Houses

Cleckheaton

Clough House

Shears Inn

St. Peter's Church, Hartshead

1 Kilometre
1 mile
Crown copyright reserved

N

a track, then in a few metres cross another stile into an old green lane. Cross the stile at the end of the track and bear half left on a clear path - single file please! -over the next field. There is a further glimpse of the Luddite landscape before you cross an awkward wooden stile and drop onto a cinder track. Turn left along it, soon bending right downhill.

'THE LUDDITE LANDSCAPE'

The Luddites were groups of cottage industry workers who banded together in an attempt to thwart the introduction of the water and steam power machinery which was replacing the various processes of cloth making by hand and hand-loom. They would maraud mostly at night. The Luddite uprising of 1812 is one theme of the novel 'Shirley', and both events and characters are visualised vividly by Charlotte who would learn of the actual happenings from her father and friends.

You reach two stiles side by side: go into the left hand field and walk down with the wall on the right to another stile at the bottom. The path continues through trees to reach New Street. Walk straight down to the main A638 road. Cross the road and turn left, then turn

right down Primrose Lane, which soon becomes an unsurfaced track. *The site of Rawfolds Mill - scene of a very unpleasant Luddite attack in 1812 - is on the right.* **Continue under the railway arch, meeting cobbles underfoot and trees overhead, and climb gently to reach a tarmac surface and a fork: keep straight forward up the unsurfaced track, and at the next fork go either left or right to arrive at the main A649 road.** *The Shears Inn is a short distance to the left.*

The Shears Inn was the headquarters of the Luddites. Visitors will be made welcome to take refreshment and learn more about the Luddite movement from old photographs and newspaper cuttings which are posted around the walls of this historic public house.

Turn right along the main road for approximately 600 metres to No.428 Halifax Road, Hightown. *This is Clough House, to which Patrick Brontë brought his young wife after their marriage in 1812. It was here that their first two children, Maria and Elizabeth, were born.* **The Way continues down Clough Lane opposite. In the dip, at the far end of the iron railings and a few metres before a bench, turn sharp right, then in a few metres left through a stile into a field. Keeping to the left hand edge of the field, climb to a small iron gate into a narrow footpath with a high wooden fence on the left. Enter the yard of Upper House Farm (beware of both nettles and dogs!) and keep straight forward between the buildings and on up the farm access road. On a tree an imposing considerate sign states 'SLOW - WALKERS CROSSING.'** *Across the fields on the right is Thornbush Farm, which was named Lousy Thorn Farm in Patrick Brontë's time - he lodged here when he first became curate of St. Peter's Church until he and Maria married in December 1812.* **At the end of the access road keep straight forward along the motor road, and when it bends left to a T-junction keep forward along the footway, cross the main road and continue forward along the footway opposite to St.Peter's Church, Hartshead,** *where Patrick Brontë was appointed curate during the time of the Luddite riots. A corner of the churchyard is said to contain unmarked graves of fated Luddite men.*

On approaching the church the Brontë Way turns right along Ladywell Road and joins the Kirklees Way, but we shall leave it here and start our return route to Oakwell Hall. So continue to the church. On the other side of the road from the entrance gate there is a footpath sign, with a mounting block and old stocks beside it. Go through the stile and walk along the edge of the field with a hedge on the right to the next stile, then bear slightly right over the next field to a wooden telegraph pole in the fence on the far side. Bear left, keeping the fence on your right. *There is a fine view right to Castle Hill, Almondbury, and the moors beyond.* Go through the stile in the next corner and keep forward, passing a gateway, with a wall on the right.

Cross the stile in the next corner and continue with the hedge/fence on your right. At the farm pass round two large metal gates and go through a small one beside a large one to follow a track past garages to the next road. Turn left along the footway. Bear left as Windy Bank Lane comes in from the right and then cross the road. Opposite Moss Cottage pass round a metal gate on the right and walk down the edge of the field with a wall on the right. At the foot of the field turn right along a cross track, in a few metres passing through a stile. The path begins to climb and you pass a cemetery. About 50 metres further on go through a stile in the wall on the left and walk straight over the field to the hedge on the far side. Pass through this and continue your line over the next field to a stile in the next hedge and a minor road.

Cross the road to the stile by the gate opposite, walk straight across two fields, half left across a third and straight across a fourth to a stile by Moorside Farm. Walk forward, cross over a track with a gate to your left to follow a fence on your left to the next stile. Turn left through the yard and walk on down a walled footpath. When you reach a metal gate with a stile beside it, go through another stile on the right and walk straight across the field to the stile in the fence opposite. Cross this and turn sharp left to follow the fence/hedge on your left. Cross the stile in the bottom corner of the field and bear very slightly right down the next very large field to the next stile in the far bottom corner.

Over this, ignore the stile on the right and turn left along a clear path with Lands Beck on your right. When you are faced by a stile in the fence ahead, ignore it and turn right to cross the beck and keep forward uphill, soon with a fence on your left. Pass through a stile and continue up the enclosed path, soon with allotments on the left. Notice on the way up a stile on the right giving access to a spring. Join a street and keep forward to the main road. You have been here before, because the Shears Inn is a short distance to the right. Cross straight over the road and follow the unsurfaced path opposite. Join a track and keep forward along it, retracing your outward route for a short distance. Ignore a street on the right. Where the track curves left 50 metres before it passes under the disused railway, fork right off it, up on to the trackbed and bear left along this.

The railway provides a 'green' route right into the centre of Cleckheaton. Follow it until just after it crosses a major road (the A643), when the path forks. Keep right, and in a few metres at another fork keep left on the better path. Soon you have the Tesco car park on your right. When you reach a gap in the fence on your right, go through it and walk straight over the car park. Pass to the left of the supermarket building and walk straight down the footway. Cross over a cross street and walk straight down Horncastle Street past the market to the main road at the bottom, cross it (this might not be too easy!) and turn left.

About 20 metres before Chapel Street turn right along the second of two unsurfaced tracks (wooden footpath sign rather concealed by vegetation), which is another former railway line. Pass through bollards and climb gently over a long viaduct. After more bollards the path bears left. Where it bears right again at a high fence, ignore it and bear left on a gently descending path with a wooden fence on the left.

At the end of the fence keep right at a faint fork, on the less clear path, along the foot of the embankment on the right. Soon you reach another wooden fence with a clear path to the right of it, which leads to a stile into a field. Follow the right hand edge until you reach a stile and a kissing-gate side by side. Go through the gate and climb steeply up the embankment of the disused railway. When the gradient eases, keep forward on a clear path, still climbing gently, with a hedge on the left. At the top of the slope the path bears slightly left along an old works fence. When the fence ends keep on by the wall on the left, join a track, pass a corner of the derelict mill, go through a gateway onto a road and turn right along the footway.

When you reach a short terrace of houses on the left, Fusden Lane comes in from the right. Keep forward, ignore Bawson Court on the left, but just after the imposing gateway into Bawson Cliffe turn left along an unsurfaced track. Pass to the right of a gate ("Beware of Dog") down a narrow enclosed footpath, and at the next house turn right and follow the access track. The track climbs to reach a motor road at a junction by Gomersal Methodist Church. Cross Latham Lane and keep forward down the road opposite. When you reach the main road (A651), cross and turn right, soon reaching the new housing development which you passed earlier. Turn left into it, but this time instead of following the access road as it bears right, fork left along a signposted ginnel which soon leads into a field.

Walk down the right hand edge of the field to the next road (A652), cross it and turn left to walk a short distance to the entrance to Oakwell Hall Country Park on the right. You can walk back up to the Hall through the Country Park, so enter the Countryside Centre car park and walk to the Information Centre at the far end. Pass to the left of it along a surfaced track. Having passed through a kissing-gate, take either branch of the path to return to your starting point.

Hartshead Church to Bailiff Bridge
Walk 2

Length of circular walk: 6¼ miles (11 km). Length of Brontë Way: 2¾ miles (4½ km). A very pleasant, mainly rural walk, on good tracks and field paths, with fine views. Much of this section of the Brontë Way coincides with the Kirklees Way, and the Calderdale Way is joined towards the end.

Map: Pathfinder 691.

Start and finish: St.Peter's Church, Hartshead (GR 189 233). There is plenty of room to park on the road outside the church. Enjoy the excellent view from the churchyard to Castle Hill, Almondbury and the moors beyond before you set off.

By bus: The 257 Dewsbury-Brighouse bus passes the church. The 218 Huddersfield-Leeds and 225 Leeds-Gomersal-Cleckheaton-Brighouse-Elland pass nearby.

Leave the churchyard and turn left along the road, **then turn left again along Ladywell Road. At the T-junction turn right. When the tarmac surface soon ends, keep on along the track. Take the first track on the left, about 40 metres before the next road. When the track bends left to Soap House Farm, go through the stile by the gate ahead and walk along the edge of the field with a fence on your left.** *Very extensive views open up ahead.* **Go through the next stile, made of rusty tin oil barrels full of concrete, and bear left down the tarmac lane. When this turns right to a gas valve house, keep forward down the path between hedges. Cross the motorway bridge and follow the track as it turns right on the far side.**

At the next junction in the dip keep left, ignoring a few metres further on a gate on the left onto the golf course. When you reach a cross track, turn right along it and follow it to the A643. Turn left along the footway for 200 metres to a stile on the right, indicated by a thick wooden post sticking up above the wall. Cross it and kink right and left to follow the fence/wall on the left to the next stile. Bear half right across the next large field towards the former railway embankment, climb this, and the next stile is visible ahead. Cross it, climb the next embankment and drop down the other side, and now aim to the right of a large pylon to reach a step-stile onto a minor road. Turn right for a few metres, then left along a farm access road. *Here we leave the Kirklees Way.*

16

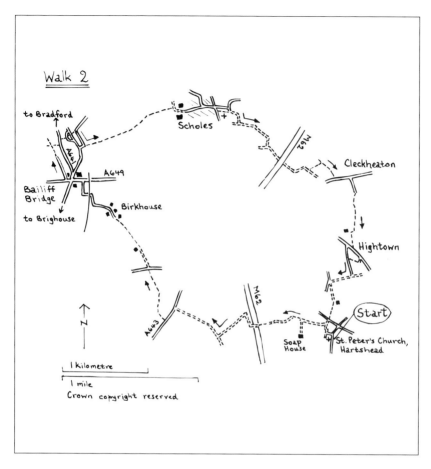

Walk 2

to Bradford
Scholes
Cleckheaton
A649
Bailiff
Bridge
Birkhouse
to Brighouse
Hightown
Start
N
Soap
House
St. Peter's Church,
Hartshead
1 Kilometre
1 mile
Crown copyright reserved

At the farm cross a cattle-grid and walk straight forward, down some steps, over a bridge and stile and keep straight forward up the next field. As you approach the next farm, bear left to a footpath sign and stile, then bear left to join a track and turn right along it. Pass to the left of the farmhouse and keep forward along the tarmac lane through Birkhouse. Follow the road downhill, with Bailiff Bridge straight ahead and Brighouse to the left. Follow the road as it turns right *(here we are joined by the Calderdale Way)* then left, to pass under the disused railway line. At the main road (A649) turn left, at the traffic lights cross straight over the Bradford to Brighouse road (A641) and just after the Punchbowl Hotel turn right along Victoria Road and follow it to its end. *It is 12 kilometres to Bailiff Bridge from the Oakwell Hall start.*

17

At the end of Victoria Road, pass round the barrier and keep forward over the rough ground. On reaching a crossing of paths a few metres before a power line pole the Brontë Way continues straight ahead, but we turn right up a grassy path with trees on the left to the main road. Cross with care and turn left, but in 70 metres, just before house no.492, turn right up a ginnel. On reaching a street, turn left for 25 metres to find the continuation of the ginnel on the right. Cross over the next street and continue up the steps and the paved path. Cross an old railway bridge and keep forward with a high fence on the right to a road. Turn right along it.

Where the road turns right, turn left along a track in the corner, which leads to a stile into a fenced path. This ends at another stile: bear slightly left over the next field to the next stile, then drop half left to cross the beck and keep forward up the other side to a stile, then on with a wall on the right to the next stile in the top corner. Bear slightly left over the next field to the next stile, then walk straight over the next field, parallel to the hedge on the left, to the next stile, and now follow the fence on your right. *At the next stile there is an extensive view back.* Now continue with the fence on your left. Cross the next stile by a gate and keep forward along the track, soon being joined by another track coming in from the left.

Pass between a school and a large factory and keep forward along a street into Scholes. When you reach a main road, bear right along the footway, but immediately after the Walkers Arms turn right down Scholes Lane. After 30 metres, opposite the post office, enter Upper Green Avenue on the left. It soon becomes a ginnel passing to the left of the church. At the end of the ginnel keep forward along Town Gate, passing a small green. Town Gate becomes Wellands Lane and curves right. Follow it to a T-junction and turn left, now along an unsurfaced track, which winds down and passes through a tunnel under the M62.

On the far side the track soon curves left and then right again, and now look out for a footpath sign pointing left. Cross the stile and walk down the edge of the field with a fence on the right to the next stile, then continue down the edge of the next field. Cross the stile in the bottom corner and the beck, then turn right and follow the fence/broken wall on your right. Cross a stile, walk forward a few metres and bear left down a tarmac road, passing to the left of St Luke's Parish Church, Cleckheaton, to reach a main road. Turn left, crossing the road when convenient, and immediately before the Ring of Bells pub turn right down the unsurfaced Brick Street.

At the bottom pass round the barrier and keep forward up the footpath over waste ground. Having passed a redundant gap-stile, take the right fork and continue uphill, keeping right when the path forks again, to stay alongside the old field boundary on the right and soon enter a path between hedges. When you draw level with Upper Blacup Farm on the right, the path turns right towards it, but just before you reach it, go up some steps on the left, through a stile, and follow the fence on the right up the edge of the field. At the top of the hill pause and enjoy the extensive view back, before continuing forward along the enclosed path, which leads to the road in Hightown almost opposite the post office.

Cross the road and turn left. Pass the Old Brown Cow and turn right along Parkin Street. In a few metres don't go through the gateway ahead but turn right along the ginnel. At the next street turn left, walk down to the bottom, pass through the bollards and turn right along the track. Follow this to the end and turn left along another track. Immediately before Thornbush Farm *(where Patrick Brontë lodged for a time)* at the end of the track cross the stile on the right and walk along the edge of the field with the farm buildings and then a fence on the left. Pass through a cross hedge and walk straight over the next field, aiming for the right hand end of a short length of hedge, to a stile out onto a road.

Cross the road and walk up the lane opposite. You will soon recognise the first track on the right, which you followed earlier. Now keep forward, turning left shortly after the tarmac surface begins and taking the next road on the right to return to Hartshead Church.

For those who would like to explore on foot more of the world of the Brontës

In the Steps of the Brontës by Eddie Flintoff

is an account of the lives and work of this gifted family arranged as a series of walks through the places they knew and loved. Several of the walks, which are all circular and vary from 3 to 10 miles in length, incorporate sections of the Brontë Way, but others move further afield, for example to Cowan Bridge, Nidderdale, Little Ouseburn, York or Scarborough, and even to the Lake District and Edinburgh.

In the Steps of the Brontës, which is published by Countryside Books at £3.95 (ISBN 1 85306 230 8) is available in local bookshops and Tourist Information Centres.

Bailiff Bridge to Shelf
Walk 3

Length of circular walk: *6½ miles (10¼ km).* *Length of Brontë Way:* *3 miles (4¾ km). A very pleasant rural ramble with fine views and some distinguished old houses. This section of the Brontë Way coincides with the Calderdale Way.*

Map: *Pathfinder 691.*

Start and finish: *Victoria Road, Bailiff Bridge. Victoria Road is alongside the Punchbowl Hotel at the main crossroads (A641/A649). Drive along it to near the end, where there is plenty of room to park on the right.*

By bus: *223/224/227 Leeds-Halifax, 363/365 Bradford-Halifax, 622/623/625 Eldwick-Bradford-Huddersfield, 626/627 Shipley-Bradford-Brighouse to the main crossroads at Bailiff Bridge.*

From the end of Victoria Road pass round the barrier and walk forward across the open ground, but when you reach the crossing of paths, keep forward to cross a footbridge and follow the clear path to a stile. Keep forward to pick up and follow a hedge on the right. The hedge becomes sparse and there are remains of a wall. Where this wall turns right, follow it and keep along the right hand edge of the next field to a stile. Walk forward across the middle of the next field to reach a gated stile and the A58 again. Cross with great care to the kissing-gate opposite and bear half left up the field, following a slight ridge.

Pass through an old field boundary and continue up the edge of the next field with a hedge on your right. At the top cross the Bradford to Halifax railway by a bridge, and keep forward, soon passing to the right of a cricket ground and catching a glimpse of Upper Rookes, a fine 17th-century hall, on the left. Walk forward across one section of the village green, passing the War Memorial on your right, then turn left at the T-junction along the Village Street of Norwood Green. *The Old White Beare Inn, which you pass on the right, was named after a galleon which took part in the fight against the Spanish Armada in 1588. The old clock tower on the left at the far end, once part of the village school, was built to mark the Silver Jubilee of Queen Victoria.*

Take the next turn right after the clock tower, along a tarmac track which soon turns into a double-paved old lane. After Middle Ox Heys Farm the track narrows to a footpath which can be overgrown in summer. At the end of the hedged section keep forward along the left hand edge of a field, passing a large pylon

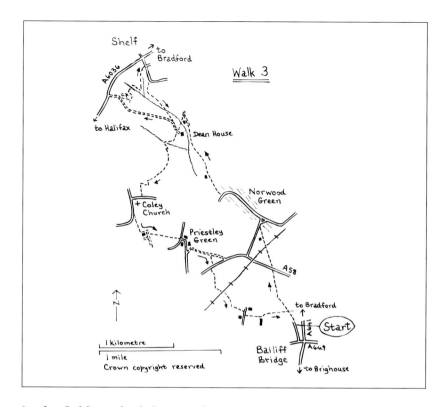

in the field on the left. Pass through a stile and go diagonally left
down the field towards the woods, then follow the clear path near
the top edge of the wood with a steep drop on the left. Ignore
paths forking left and keep along the upper path to Heathwood
House. 50 metres past the house turn left down a long flight of
stone steps to cross the stream via a wooden footbridge.

Cross the stile into a field and bear left, heading for the right
hand end of a stone barn at Dean House Farm, cross the stile and
turn right up the access road. Follow this track to Shelf. When the
ground levels off at Shelf Hall Park, the Brontë Way continues
forward along an unmade lane called Bridle Stile to the A6036, but
circular walkers should turn sharp right into the car park. Leave it again
through a gap in the fence in the bottom left hand corner and follow the
path down through the trees and down the steps. Pass through the
gateway and turn left and left again to walk along a tarmac drive with
tennis courts and bowling green on the right. There are public toilets
here. Follow the drive as it curves left, but a few metres after you pass
the end of the wood on the left turn right to walk down the grass (no

path), passing between a holly tree and a sycamore, and on reaching the wood you will see that you are being led down a flight of steps into it.

Cross the footbridge at the bottom and bear right with the path. After a time the path curves left away from the beck and climbs a slope over waste ground. Re-enter the trees and there is another beck down on your right. Follow the path to a kissing-gate and a road and turn right along the footway. Where this ends just after a post box, go through the kissing-gate on the right and follow the path descending into the wood. At a fork keep right on the stepped descending path, soon reaching the beck, which you keep on your right for a time, before crossing it by a sleeper bridge. Follow the path up the other side, soon entering a field through a gap in the fence. The path leads along a field edge to a track Turn left along it. You've been here before!

A few metres before the gate into the farmyard of Dean House Farm turn right through a stile by a gate and walk along the edge of the field with a hedge/fence on your left to reach a stile into a wood. Follow the path down into the wood, in a few metres keeping right at a fork. Cross the beck at the bottom by a footbridge and climb the other side, but ignore a flight of steps straight ahead and fork left immediately after a bench to follow another flight of steps up through the wood. The path leaves the wood by a stile with a massive pylon in the field on the left.

Follow the wall on your left for a few metres, then go through a stile on the left and keep following another wall on the left to pass under the pylon. Cross the stile ahead, pass through an old gate, and keep forward along the left hand edge of the next field, which is quite narrow, and you soon pass through the remains of the next hedgerow by an old stone stile. Now bear half right across the next field to the left hand end of a gap in the hedge opposite, aiming to the left of the tower of Coley Church in the distance. In the dip there is another gate and stone stile, and now continue your line diagonally up the next field, heading directly for the church tower and passing under the power lines.

On reaching the power lines, the path on the ground keeps straight forward, but the right of way actually bears slightly right to a wall corner, passes through a stile in the corner, immediately followed by a large wooden gate, and follows the wall on the left up the field. At the top turn left through a stile, and now follow the wall on your right as far as the next corner. Here go through a stile on the right and follow the left hand edge of the next field. At the end of this field ignore the gap-stile in the wall ahead and turn left through the stile by the gateway to follow a wall on your right to the next stile. Continue along the right hand edge of the next field to reach a lane. Turn right along it, pass Coley Church and turn left at the motor road.

When the road bears right, keep forward along a grassy track to cross a stile by a gate, then continue with the wall/fence on your left. *The view right is to Halifax, straight ahead over Hipperholme towards Brighouse.* Turn left through a kissing-gate into a walled track which leads along the back of Wynteredge Hall. At the end turn right for a few metres, but where the wall on the left ends cross the stile by the gate on the left and bear half right down the field, parallel to the power lines, and looking back for a view of the superb 17th-century hall. Pass between two old gateposts and continue your line down the next field to a double stile at the bottom of the field. Walk straight down the next field, keeping to the right of a row of trees, to cross another double stile and reach the road at Priestley Green.

Cross the road diagonally right and walk down Syke Lane opposite. *Prior's Mead is a fine 17th-century hall on the left.* The road curves right past some more attractive cottages. At the end of the wall on the left turn back left along a track. Follow this until you reach a stile in the fence on the right: it comes just after a section where there have been fields on both sides of the track and just before the track becomes hedged on both sides. Cross the stile and walk slightly left across the field to reach the A58 over another stile. Turn right for 25 metres, then cross this busy road with great care to the stile opposite, which gives access to a golf course.

Walk straight down the grass, soon with trees on the left, cross the beck by a broad bridge and follow the gravel track up the other side. The right of way across the golf course is marked by wooden posts painted red. Beware of flying golf balls as you cross several fairways. When the gravel ends, keep forward to the next wooden post and walk along to the right of a hedge. The red posts lead you to a cross hedge. Turn left and follow the hedge, then wall, on your right, and when the wall ends, keep forward to re-cross the railway by a sleepered crossing (care!).

On the far side cross the field to the stile opposite, then cross the next field to the next stile. Now bear half right to a large wooden gate in the wall at the corner of the cricket ground, but don't go through it, instead bear left and walk along the edge of the field with the wall on your right. Cross the stile in the corner and enter a fenced path which leads to a tarmac lane. Turn right for a short distance, but immediately before the next house on the right turn left through a stile and walk along the left hand edge of the field. At the far end cross a stile and follow a track forward past the end of a terrace of cottages. Where the track turns right again, go left through a kissing-gate into a field and keep forward on a grassy track which soon bears right and descends to cross a beck by a stone bridge. Keep forward until you reach a cross path and turn right to reach the end of Victoria Road.

Shelf to Thornton
Walk 4

Length of circular walk: 9 miles (14½ km). *Length of Brontë Way:* 4¼ miles (6¾ km). *Field paths and old tracks through undulating pastoral countryside with good views.*

Maps: Pathfinder 691, 682.

Start and finish: The car park of Shelf Hall Park. On the A6036 Bradford to Halifax road, at the Halifax end of Shelf Hall Park, there is a lane called Bridle Stile. Drive down this to a fork with a lamppost in the middle and bear left into the car park.

By bus: Take the 571 Bradford-Halifax or the 570 Bradford-Sowerby Bridge bus from Bradford Interchange to Shelf Hall Park.

Walk up Bridle Stile to the main road and cross it to a cobbled snicket/ginnel directly opposite. At the top of this cross the road and turn left. The "official" route of the Brontë Way crosses Broad Ings Way and a few metres further on turns right along the signposted footpath into a farmyard, there bearing right to pass between a barn and a wooden fence. Leave the yard again and keep forward along the track, with school playing fields to the left. At the end of the houses on the right, where the track turns sharp right, cross the stile ahead to the right of the gate. Now after wet weather this track can be excessively muddy, so if you prefer a drier route, turn right along Broad Ings Way into the new housing estate. Turn left up Park Stone Rise and at the top pass the prominent white bollard into a tarmac footpath. Mount two concrete steps to climb over the wall and jump steeply onto the track, turn left and follow the track up to the corner where you turn right through a stile on the right of a large metal gate. Now the two routes have joined up again. Follow a broken stone wall on the left for two fields. At the end of the second field continue between two stone gateposts and along the track, with the wall now on the right. At the end of this field cross the stile at the side of rather an ornate metal gate and turn right along the track.

At the tarmac road, Giles Hill Lane, turn left for a few metres, then take the first road on the right, Brackens Lane. Just before a narrow strip of woodland a public footpath sign points left along a double walled path. At the end cross the stile and keep forward with a wall on the left. Where the field begins to drop to

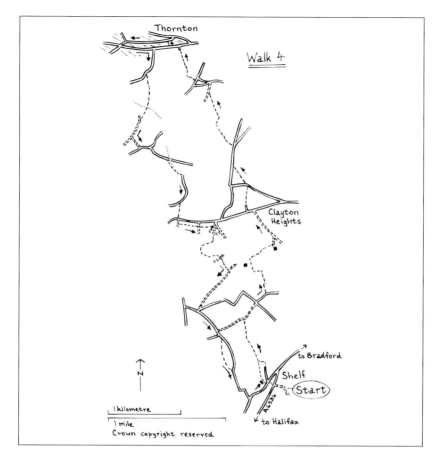

Thornton

Walk 4

Clayton Heights

to Bradford

Shelf

Start

N

1 kilometre

1 mile

Crown copyright reserved

to Halifax

A6036

Blackshaw Beck, cross a wooden stile by the gate on the left and follow the fence on your left for about 20 metres, before following a clear path descending to cross the beck by the first of the two bridges. Cross the stile and walk up the field with a wall on the left. In the top corner cross the stile and walk straight across the middle of the next field, with Bobby Green Farm to the left, to the stile opposite. Keep forward to cut the corner of the next field to a stile in the wall on the right.

Walk along the edge of the next field with a wall on the left. Cross the stile in the next corner and bear slightly left to the next stile. Walk straight over the next field on a paved path to a wall corner, then along to the left of a small wood to a stile onto a walled track. Turn left and follow it to the A647 at Clayton Heights.

Cross the road and turn left for about 80 metres, then directly opposite Clayton Heights Methodist church turn right along Sheep Hill Lane. *(If refreshment is required, the Old Dolphin public house is a short distance further along the main road. A frequent bus service runs on the A647 into Bradford City. At the A647 just over 19 kilometres have been walked from the start.)* The track narrows to a footpath, *and on crossing the brow of the hill there is a fine view half left to Thornton village across the picturesque Pinchbeck valley. Thornton viaduct can also be seen in the distance to the left of the village. It carried the now disused Halifax/Keighley railway across the valley.*

THE BIRTHPLACE VILLAGE

Cross over the next metalled road to the footpath opposite, which soon bends left and follows a wall on the right downhill. At the foot of the slope cross the farm track and continue straight down the middle of the next field to the next stile, then straight across the next field to the public footpath sign, stile and main road. Cross the road and turn right along the footway into Clayton. Just after crossing Brook Lane, which comes in from the left, and immediately before a post box and some wooden benches, a Brontë Way sign points left along a tarmac drive to a large wooden gate. Pass through the gap beside this gate. When the garden fences on the right end, ignore a cross path and keep forward through a stile and down the edge of the field with a wall on the left.

There is another excellent view of Thornton straight ahead. Go through the stile in the bottom corner of the field and turn sharp right to follow the wall on the right. The wall curves left and there is a stile in it just before a gate. Cross this and immediately turn left through another stile, then walk down the edge of the field with the wall on the left. Pass through the stile in the bottom corner and continue downhill still with the wall on the left. When the wall ends, keep forward to pass to the right of the power line pole, and soon the broken wall resumes. When you reach an old gateway in this wall on the left (you have a short stretch of wall blocking the way ahead) kink left, then right through it and continue down to join a track which has been descending through the field from the left. Turn right down this and follow it to the next motor road.

Turn left and at the fork keep left along the ONE WAY section, then turn right at the T-junction and take the first track on the left. In a few metres don't fork right into the tarmac yard, but pass

OLD
BELL CHAPEL
THORNTON

BRONTE
BIRTHPLACE
THORNTON

through the stile on the right of the large metal gate and follow the track which soon bends right and passes to the left of **Rayners Cornmill Farm** - *you may be greeted by barking dogs here-* **then cross a stile by a gate and continue up the track. Don't go through the next gate but pass to the right of it to find a stile in the wall on the left. Bear slightly left and climb towards the tall trees at the top of the slope, crossing one, or maybe two stiles on the way. Eventually you are following a hedge/fence on your left up to the top corner to reach a kissing gate.** *Pause on the way up to look back for the view to Clayton Heights.* **Turn left and quick right at the side of Thornton Hall Farm up a track to the main B6145.**

Turn left along the road. *In the wall on the left is a metal gate which is the way into the churchyard and the listed ruined remains of the Old Bell Chapel where Patrick Brontë preached from 1815-20.* **Cross the road to St. James's Parish Church.** *Contact Revd Stuart Hacking (01274-833200) if you wish to look inside, where the font and copies of the baptismal certificates of the Brontë children can be seen.* **Just**

DETAIL OF WALL PLAQUE

past the main porch of the church a footpath sign pointing to the right leads up a narrow snicket at the side of the church. Turn left along Brontë Old Road, which becomes Market Street. Hesitate a little while outside numbers 72 and 74 Market Street.

This is where it all began! This is the Old Parsonage and birthplace of the four famous Brontë children. Note the plaque on the wall for the birth dates. This was Patrick's first real Parish Parsonage when he and Maria, with their two elder daughters Maria and Elizabeth, arrived in May 1815. During their residence here Patrick wrote two books which were published. These were perhaps the inspiration that led to his children becoming famous writers. Patrick was reputed to have said that some of his happiest days were spent at Thornton. They lived here for five years until their departure to Haworth in April 1820. It is hoped that from 1998 there will be limited public access to the house.

At the end of Market Street the Brontë Way forks right up West Lane, but to return to Shelf fork left down Kipping Lane. Cross over the main road and continue down Lower Kipping Lane for a short distance to view Kipping House on the left. *(Kipping House was the home of the Firth family who were close friends of the Brontës and godparents to Elizabeth and Anne).* Now return to the main road and turn right. A short distance along on the right is South Square, *a group of twelve tastefully renovated early nineteenth century workers cottages, now a busy community offering art and craft workshops, a bookshop and a restaurant/teashop (South Square Café is open Tuesday-Saturday 10.30-4.30, Sunday 12.00-4.00 for home baking and vegetarian meals).*

Continue along the main road, then just before the start of the 40mph limit turn right down Green Lane, leading to Headley Lane. The road descends, crosses Pinch Beck and passes a terrace of houses on the left. Just where it begins to climb again, ascend a flight of stone steps on the left, which lead to an enclosed footpath. Cross the stile at the far end of this and walk foward along the left hand edge of the paddock to the next stile, cross over a new road, then another stile, then keep following the wall on the left past a ruined building into and up the next field. Stone steps lead up to the next stile, from which you keep straight up the next field on the line of an old field boundary marked at first by large trees.

At the top more steps lead up to the next stile, from which you continue with the wall on your left. The next set of steps, rather the worse for wear, leads up to the top of the railway embankment. A bridge leads over the former railway and you enter an enclosed footpath. When the fence on the right ends, keep following the wall on the left to the next stile, then keep forward up the farm track. As you approach the buildings of West Scholes, look out for a double walled track on the left and follow it to the next motor road. Cross and turn left along the footway, then take the first minor road forking right, Brow Lane.

Immediately before the road passes under the railway viaduct cross the stile by the gate on the right and walk up the track. When you reach the old railway line, bear right along it. *On the left is the site of the former Queensbury Station.* Follow the main track as it curves left *(the track straight ahead here used to carry the line to Halifax through the Queensbury Tunnel)* to reach a tarmac lane and walk up this. Ignore various footpath signs on both sides of the road, until a few metres after a signposted path on the right with an ornate iron gate at the start a signpost on the left points up a double walled lane. Climb steeply up this - it can be overgrown in summer, and be careful not to trip over stones which have fallen from the walls - and look back for a last sight of Thornton before you reach the A647 in Queensbury.

Cross straight over and follow the unmade road opposite. Just before you reach a gate across this road, turn left along another track. The track narrows to a tarmac ginnel which crosses various streets and ends at a road. Cross this and take the enclosed footpath opposite, with a wood on the right. After a time the path crosses an access drive with an imposing gateway on the right and ends at an unsurfaced lane. Turn right, in a few metres forking left, but when you reach another unsurfaced track on the right, turn along it. Shortly after another track has joined you from the right, go through a wooden kissing-gate on the left by a Nature Trail sign. Follow the path down into a field *(there is a comfortable picnic table on the left)* and bear right along a broad grassy path.

The path bends right, and left, and very sharp right, and left again, and when you reach a large grassy area with another Nature Trail sign on the right, turn sharp left, still on your broad grassy track, which soon bears left again. Do you have the impression that you are walking round in circles?! Just before the broad path turns sharp left again, look for and take a narrow footpath forking right, which leads in about 50 metres to a stile in a wall. Pass through° this and walk straight forward diagonally across the track to a stile on the right just to the right of a metal gate. Go through this and walk down the edge of the field with a wall on your left. Follow this wall down and round to the next corner, where a stile gives access to a track. Turn right along it. *Soon you pass Queensbury Golf Course on your right.*

At the next motor road bear right, but take the first minor road on the left, High Cross Lane. After a time you cross a tarmac road on the right, then pass an Edward VII postbox on the right. Follow the next footpath sign which points half right along an unsurfaced track. Pass through a stile by a gate, keep forward along the track, pass through another stile by a gate and keep on with the wall on your left, now in a pathless field. Cross the stile in the next corner and keep on by the wall. In this field look out for a gated stile in the wall, go through it and turn right, keeping along the top of the bank, soon with a wooden fence on your right. Just before a metal gate in this fence cross the stile on the right and walk forward, bearing left through a gate and down a track to a stile by another gate and so back out onto the road. Turn right and follow the road down to Shelf. At the T-junction turn left and walk along the footway until you reach the ginnel on the right, marked by a Calderdale Way sign, which you used at the start of the walk. Go down it, cross the main road at the foot and continue along Bridle Stile opposite to return to your car.

Thornton to Denholme
Walk 5

Length of circular walk: 7½ miles (12 km). _Length of Brontë Way:_ 3½ miles (5¼ km). Field paths and tracks through a pastoral landscape, with excellent views. The walk is well provided with pubs!

Maps: Pathfinder 682; most of the walk is on Outdoor Leisure 21.

Start and finish: Junction of Market Street, Kipping Lane and West Lane in the centre of Thornton. There is on-street parking either on the main Thornton Road or on the wider sections of West Lane.

By bus: 503 Bradford-Huddersfield, 607 Bradford-Thornton, 696/697 Bradford-Keighley, 698/699 Bradford-Haworth-Oxenhope to Thornton.

At the end of Market Street the Brontë Way forks right in front of the Black Horse pub up West Lane. At the T-junction at the top turn right for a few metres, then left along Reservoir View. At the far end go through an opening in the wall and over a wooden step-stile to walk along the edge of a field with a fence on the right. At the end of the field cross a wooden stile and then a stone gap-stile and walk straight across the next field. Pass through another gap-stile, and now you have a wall on the left. Cross another stile and keep by the wall to the next stile, then walk straight over the next field to a kissing-gate into Thornton Cemetery. The broad tarmac drive straight through the cemetery leads to another kissing gate at the far end.

Walk along the back of some cottages, pass through a stile and bear right up a track, cobbled at first. After an uphill climb of 100 metres, a waymark post on the left indicates a wall stile onto an old paved field path to the right of a wall. Pass through an old field boundary and keep forward, keeping to the right of a wooden marker post, and right of a broken wall to a gap-stile in the corner of the field. Now the wall is on your right. Pass through another stile and keep by the wall. When you reach the houses, pass through a gap on the right of a metal gate, walk forward along a raised pavement, go through a wooden gate and turn right up a track.

At the main road the White Horse Inn is a short distance to the right. Cross the road and turn left, but just after cottage no. 16 turn right through a stile, and at the end of the wall on the left

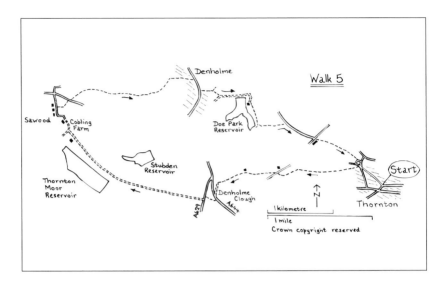

bear rather more than half left and walk over the field to a gap-stile visible in the wall ahead. *The wind turbines on Ovenden Moor are prominent ahead.* Cross the stile and bear very slightly right across the next field to the next stile. *A glorious view opens up right to Rombalds Moor, Little and Great Whernside, Simon's Seat and the fells of Upper Wharfedale.* Cross the stile and again bear slightly right to the next one. *Doe Park Reservoir is down to the right: we shall have a closer look at it later on the circular walk.* Keep your line over the next field to the farm. Cross the stile by the corner of the shed with a rusty corrugated iron roof, turn left along the concrete access road for a few metres, then cross a wooden stile on the right, to the right of a large metal gate.

The path now bears half left down the next field and crosses a stile in the wall beside a wooden telegraph pole. Bear slightly right to the next stile, which is 12 metres to the left of a gap in the wall in the field corner. Cross the stile and follow the wall on your right. Cross the stile in the next corner and continue with the wall/fence on your right. *The spire of Denholme Church is visible right.* Cross the next stile and keep on with the wall/fence on the right. The next stile leads into a narrow path between fence and wall. When the fence meets a wall, turn sharp left, keeping the wall on your left. Turn right in the next corner and follow the wall down to a stile in the bottom corner of the field. Bear left along the path, with Denholme Beck on your right.

32

Join an access drive and bear left up it to the A644. Bear left along the footway, crossing the road when convenient, and turn up the first tarmac lane on the right, Cragg Lane. In a few metres turn right up a ginnel between houses, and when the houses end, bear half left uphill with a wall to your right. In the next corner of the field cross the stile and follow the wall on your left up to the A629 Halifax to Keighley road. Cross diagonally left and walk up Black Edge Lane on the right.

This double walled track climbs gently, *and as you rise, fine views open up to the right, and half left the wind turbines are visible again. After a time Stubden Reservoir comes into view down on the right, with Denholme behind it, and you pass the embankment of Thornton Moor Reservoir up on the left.* **Having passed to the right of a small wood and a large house with an interesting stone air-shaft in its garden and passed round a large metal gate, ignore a tarmac road on the right and keep straight on to the next junction. Here the Brontë Way curves left with the road,** but our return route to Thornton lies to the right through the small metal gate beside the large double gate along an unsurfaced track signposted to Sawood.

The lane becomes tarmac and begins to descend and curve left, *and there is a splendid view of Leeming Reservoir and Oxenhope.* The road bends right and drops through the attractive old houses of Sawood. Continuing straight down this road would bring you to the Dog and Gun pub at the bottom, but we follow the first footpath sign on the right through a large metal gate and up a rough field with a wall on the left. Cross what I take to be a broken stile on the left of a large gate at the top and immediately turn right to climb another rusty gate, then turn left along the edge of the next field with a wall/fence to your left. You have to negotiate another rusty gate to reach the B6141. Cross straight over to the signposted stile opposite and walk gently uphill with a dilapidated wall on your left.

Follow the wall up to where it meets a much better wall. Cross the stile on the left and continue your line, now with the wall on your right. *The views to the left from this path are superb: Haworth and Keighley are visible, Airedale and the woods around Bingley.* Follow the wall until a gated stile gives access to a short stretch of walled lane, at the end of which go through the stile on the left and continue with the wall/fence on your right. At the end of this long field pass through the stile, and now the wall is on your left. Follow the wall through this field and three more, cross over the end of a walled lane, go through a metal gate into the next field and walk along at first with the wall on your right, then gradually bearing left away from it over to the far left hand corner of the field.

Cross a metal ladder-stile, bear right for a few metres to a gated stile, then follow the path forward through the heather along the top of Denholme Edge. Follow the path straight on and down, eventually as a hollow way with a wall on the right. Join a track and follow it down to the busy A629 in Denholme. *The Black Bull is across the road to the left.* Turn right along the footway and cross the road when convenient. Just after Hill Crest Road on the right go through a gap in the wall on the left to find a good path descending with a garden fence on the right. When the fence ends, keep forward, soon between hedges. Cross straight over a street and continue down the path opposite. When you are faced by a fence, with a stile on the left, turn right and follow the fence on your left down to a tarmac lane.

Bear left down the lane. At the bottom of the hill walk straight across the dam of Doe Park Reservoir, then follow the track as it turns right. When the track descends to a house, fork left off it to a stile by a gate and keep forward on the lowest path, parallel to the side of the reservoir. When you are faced by a wall, cross the stile in it and turn left to follow the wall on your left to a stile into the wood. Cross this (the next few metres can be excessively muddy) and follow the path straight up through the wood, to leave it again by another stile at the top. Bear slightly right over the field to the next stile, then cross to the far side of the next field, which is quite narrow at this point, and bear left uphill, keeping the wall on your right. Pass to the right of the pylon, go through the stile at the top of the field and out onto a road.

Turn right and follow the road. When it forks just before a T-junction, keep left. *The terrace of houses opposite is called Moscow.* Cross the main road diagonally left into an unsurfaced track opposite, with a terrace of houses to the right of it. When the short track ends, pass through the stile and follow the wall on your right along another old path which has been paved at one time. Keep the wall on your right through several fields, until you pass through a stile and find the wall now on your left. Follow this wall to the next road. Immediately opposite is the Sun Inn. Turn left the short distance to the junction, then go right down West Lane. Follow the footway down past the junction with Hill Top Road, bearing left down West Lane to return to the centre of Thornton.

Denholme to Haworth
Walk 6

Length of circular walk: 6¼ miles (11 km). Length of Brontë Way: 3½ miles (5½ km). Fine views, attractive landscape and many pleasant houses. A delightful round.

Map: Outdoor Leisure 21.

Start and finish: Haworth. Use one of the car parks and make your way to the Tourist Information Centre, from where the walk description starts. Attractions in Haworth village include The Brontë Parsonage Museum, St. Michael and all Angels Church, the cobbled Main Street and the Keighley and Worth Valley Railway. The Black Bull is famous as the Brontë son Branwell's 'local'. His chair stands on the staircase of the pub.

By train: Worth Valley line from Keighley.

By bus: 663/664/665/698/699 from Bradford, 720 from Keighley.

Walk down the cobbled main street with its many gift shops and cafés. About half way down, opposite the Fleece Inn, fork left down a steep cobbled lane (signposted Toilets and Railway Station), cross the main road at the bottom and either continue straight down Butt Lane or, more attractively, fork right into the park. Keep heading downhill and you will arrive at a children's playground by a paddling pool. From the pool continue down the steps and the tarmac path, then down another flight of steps. Whichever route down you choose, turn right along the road at the bottom, passing the Bygone Days Museum, and on reaching the main road, cross and turn left to cross the bridge over the beck and the railway. When the main road turns left as Station Road, turn right along Brow Road.

Immediately after the road bends left turn right up some steps and follow the flagged path by a high wall. The clear path leads up the valley of Bridgehouse Beck, negotiating various kissing-gates, crossing an iron footbridge and passing through iron bollards. In the field before the path reaches a ruined house ignore a path forking right to cross the beck by a footbridge and keep straight forward, soon with a fence to your right, to pass to the right of the ruin and reach a stile in the wall corner ahead. Follow the fence/wall on your right and bear right along a track in front of a house. At the far end of the garden pass through a gate and immediately turn right down the remains of an old walled lane.

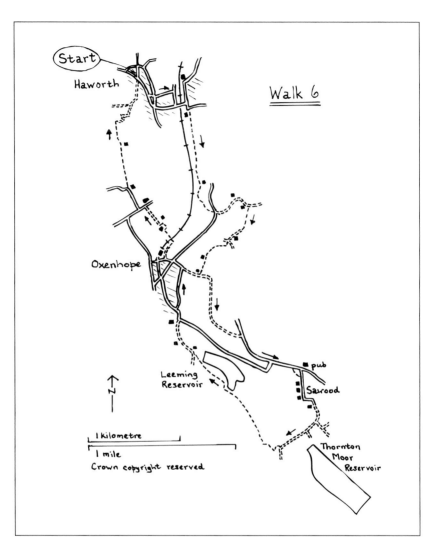

Walk 6

Haworth

Oxenhope

N

Leeming
Reservoir

pub

Sawood

Thornton
Moor
Reservoir

1 kilometre

1 mile

Crown copyright reserved

When you reach a stone packhorse bridge, do not cross, but stand with your back to it and head half right over the field, soon passing through the remains of an old wall, making for the top right hand corner - there is no clear path. Three metres to the left of this corner cross through the broken wall and immediately turn right through a gap-stile where a fence coming down the hillside meets the wall. A clear path climbs steeply through the wood to reach the road up some steps. Cross diagonally right (care, because visibility is poor!) and walk up the track opposite.

On reaching Upper Royd Barn the track bears right and becomes grassy. Pass through a gate and continue along the track. *There is a lovely view right to Oxenhope and the moors beyond.* Pass through another gate and keep forward up a tarmac access drive *(we have now joined the Worth Way),* but a few metres after the tarmac ends go through a gap-stile in the wall on the right and bear half right past a fence corner to pick up a path contouring left to pass some gorse bushes. Pass through a broken wall then slant gently right to pick up and follow a wall/fence on the right which leads in a few metres to a gap-stile by a gate. Continue with the wall on the right, then cross a stile by a gate on the right into a walled lane which leads down to a house.

Pass to the right of the house and walk down the access track. Immediately after a tarmac track comes in from the left, fork left off the track and follow a wall on your left to a rather well-hidden stile into a field. Follow the hedge on the left along: it becomes a wall, which soon bends right and leads to a gap-stile in the next corner. Bear half right over the next field to a stile beside a gate and walk along the walled lane to Lower Hayley Farm. Walk straight past the left hand end of the farm, through a gate, along the left hand edge of a small field, through a stile and on with the wall on the left to the next stile, which leads into an enclosed path which passes to the left of a white house to reach a tarmac lane. *Here we leave the Worth Way.*

Turn left up the lane. Soon there are more fine views over Oxenhope to the moors. After passing some houses the lane begins to climb again, and Leeming Reservoir is down below on the right. Follow the lane to a minor road, bear right along this and follow it down to the main Oxenhope to Denholme road. Turn left up this, being careful because there is no footway. *It is not far now to the Dog and Gun, almost half way round our walk and a suitable refreshment stop.* After leaving the pub, the walk continues up the minor road opposite. If you don't want to visit the pub, you can cut a corner by crossing the stile on the right about 150 metres before the pub and bearing half left over the field to the next stile, then continue half left up the next field to a stile out onto the lane just below Sawood. Bear right up the lane.

Soon you will recognise the route of Walk 5. After the tarmac ends at Cobling Farm keep on along the track, pass through the small metal gate beside the large double gate and keep forward up the tarmac road. You have now rejoined the route of the Brontë Way. **When the tarmac road curves left through a gate to Thornton Moor Reservoir, keep straight forward along the track.** *There is a fine view right to Leeming*

Reservoir and Oxenhope. **Go through a gate and continue along the track. Just before the wall on the left turns left, a wooden signpost opposite points you right down a grassy path which soon curves left and drops into what used to be a walled lane.**

Walk straight down the slope, following an old wall, for about 150 metres, then when you reach a tall isolated sycamore tree on the right turn sharp left (a waymark on an old stone gatepost points the way) for 40 metres, then at a marker post turn sharp right again and continue downhill - you should keep in the old walled lane, but this is so overgrown that most walkers keep to the left of it - and when the walled lane ends, bear slightly right down to a high ladder-stile. You cross a deep culvert at this point. Continue downhill with the wall on the right to a stile in the next corner, then straight down the next field and into the next one, where again you have a wall on the right.

Follow this down to the next stile, under trees, then continue with a high fence on your right, before bearing left downhill away from the fence to cross the remains of a stile in a wall corner with a beck on your left. Bear left over the bridge, then immediately right on a clear path with trees on your right and the beck below. When the trees end, bear slightly left and drop to a wall corner. Pass to the left of this, cross a wooden footbridge and bear right along the wall on your right. Go through a stile and keep on with the wall on your right for a short distance, then a fence, to the next stile, and now you have a wall on your left. The reservoir is over to the right.

Cross the next stile into a short section of enclosed path, then climb a step-stile and continue with the fence/wall on your right to join a farm access road. Bear right down this. *Haworth appears half right in the distance.* **When you reach a fork, with the right hand branch heading along below the reservoir dam, keep straight forward down an enclosed footpath. Bear right past a house, and keep on down the paved path and then the track. When the track joins a road keep forward down it, and on reaching the main road through Oxenhope cross to the footway opposite and turn left. Take the first street on the right past the post office, Yate Lane. Having passed the fine old manor house, the road curves left and climbs. Keep forward along this narrow road to a T-junction and turn left down to the main road.**

Cross the road and turn left for a few metres, then right down Harry Lane. When the road curves left as Mill Lane, fork right along a track. *(Refreshments are available in the charming environment of a converted railway carriage at Oxenhope Station during the hours when trains are running, i.e. every day at holidays and in summer, at weekends all year. To reach the station continue along Mill Lane and turn right down Station Road.)* Pass to the left of a house, after which the track narrows to a footpath and enters a field, soon with the beck down on the left. Cross the beck by a footbridge, ignore the walled path on the right and cross the step-stile ahead, turn sharp right and then left over the railway (care!), then bear left up to a stile on the right and walk steeply up the slope with a wall on the left.

We have now joined the Railway Children Walk, and the house at the top of the slope over the wall is Bents Farm, otherwise Three Chimneys, the home of the Railway Children. Follow the wall round to the right of the house, cross the stile and turn left past the house, then right up the access road. Turn left at the next motor road, then right up Old Oxenhope Lane. Where the road bends left at Old Oxenhope Farm turn right into the farmyard then immediately left past a large stone trough to follow the wall on your left up to a stile by a gate. Keep on by the wall, soon entering a narrow walled lane by a gap-stile. When this ends the wall is now on your right. Cross a stile and the bottom of a broad walled lane and keep on by the wall on your right.

Cross a stile just before some renovated houses and bear left, keeping a wall on your left. On reaching an access road, cross diagonally right to take the left hand of the two stiles, a small metal gate with a notice saying "Bull in Field". Walk straight across the field, soon with a wall on your right. When your way ahead is blocked by a wall, turn right down a walled path. Follow this as it bends left, then right, then left again, and on the next stretch look out for a junction where the Brontë Way turns left up a walled lane (a stile by a gate on the right gives access to a car park and picnic area), but no one will want to omit a visit to Haworth, so keep forward into the village. For the Parsonage and Church take the path to the left of the church, for the village centre and our starting point pass to the right of it.

Haworth to Ponden Reservoir
Walk 7

Length of circular walk: 6¼ miles (10¼ km). _Length of Brontë Way:_ 3¼ miles (5¼ km). The inclusion of Top Withins ('Wuthering Heights'), which does not form part of the Brontë Way, will add another 2¼ miles (3½ km) to the circuit. Fine moorland walking with excellent views, and an attractive crossing of the Worth valley.

Map: Outdoor Leisure 21.

Start and finish: Hare Hill Edge picnic site, on the road from Oakworth to Laneshaw Bridge, 350 metres west of the Grouse Inn, at GR 007 384, marked by a large layby and a couple of picnic tables. Do try to fit in a visit to the Grouse Inn, a lovely old Timothy Taylor pub of great charm with a landlord who is a real 'character'.

By train: Worth Valley line from Keighley to Haworth.

By bus: 663/664/665/698/699 from Bradford, 720 from Keighley to Haworth. In both cases start the walk at [*].

'WUTHERING HEIGHTS'

Walk along the road in the Oakworth direction, but opposite the entrance to the first house on the left cross the stile on the right and walk down the field with the fence/wall on your left. You reach Oldfield Lane by a telephone kiosk. Turn left along the road and enjoy the fine view over the Worth valley. After about 500 metres turn right over a cattle-grid by a short length of breeze block wall and walk down the track. When it begins to curve right, fork left off it and follow the fence on your left down to a stile by a large rusty gate. Cross this and walk forward a few metres to join the access road to Street Head Farm. Turn right along it, but immediately take the left fork and walk along the left hand edge of the yard to a stile by a gate into an area of grass with scattered young trees, actually an old walled lane. The path develops into a hollow way which descends through trees to reach a ladder-stile.

Keep forward, passing a deep ravine on the right, and cross another stile into the continuation of the walled lane. When this ends at another ladder-stile, keep forward down its line, cross over a farm track which leads through a gate on the left, and walk down the left hand edge of the next field. You bend left as you near the foot. Go

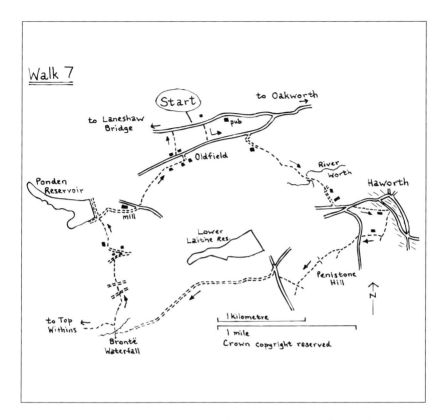

Walk 7

through a gap beside a large metal gate and walk forward with the River Worth on your left, then cross it by a lovely old packhorse bridge. Turn right up the track. Cross a stile and keep on up the old lane. Soon it bends slightly right uphill and becomes very overgrown, so walk up the field edge to the right of it to a ladder-stile by Lower Oldfield Farm.

Walk a few steps forward and turn right up the track. Pass to the right of the end of a terrace of cottages and continue up the track, bearing left with it when it becomes tarmac to reach a road. Bear left into Haworth. Another road comes in from the right, and 60 metres further on, just past a bus stop on the right, go through a stile on the right and follow a paved path which the Brontës must have known well over the field. Go through another stile and pass some modern houses to reach a cobbled street which leads past the Brontë Parsonage Museum. *The old Schoolroom, which you also pass, may be open for refreshments.*

[*] **To continue the Brontë Way turn right immediately before the church on a cobbled path through the churchyard. Where the cobbles end, kink left down some steps, then right along a paved path. When the paving ends at a path junction, a signpost points you right up a walled lane. At the next road cross straight over and bear half left on a clear track into Penistone Hill Country Park. When the track forks, keep right, and a short distance further on bear right with the main track.** *Can you see your car across the valley?* **At the next path crossing again take the right fork, i.e. keep straight forward** - *Lower Laithe Reservoir is now visible half right* - **and at the next fork, before some tumbled boulders, keep right on the broader path. On reaching a car park, keep forward along its right hand edge and down the access track, but on reaching a junction of tracks turn right down a signposted footpath across the moor.**

On reaching a road, cross straight over to the path opposite. It leads down to a track. Turn left through the kissing-gate beside the cattle-grid and follow the track all the way to the Brontë Waterfall. *Look out for the point where the wall on the right finally ends, just after you cross a sleeper bridge, because from here, if you look up to the head of the valley, just to the right of the valley near the top, you will see a solitary tree and a cluster of ruins. This is Top Withins ('Wuthering Heights').*

On reaching the falls *(in Emily Brontë's time this would have been a secluded area where she walked with her dog Keeper to write poems and glean inspiration for her novel 'Wuthering Heights')* **cross the beck by the bridge and climb steeply up to a kissing-gate.** *From around here is perhaps the best view of the waterfall. Now you must choose whether to include Top Withins in your walk. If you decide to do so, after the kissing-gate take the left fork on a new section of paved and stepped path. Your goal is in sight most of the way and a clear path leads directly to it. The ruined Top Withins is traditionally but incorrectly known as 'Wuthering Heights', the home of the Earnshaws and Heathcliff in Emily Brontë's novel. After your visit, return by the same route to the kissing-gate.* **To continue the Brontë Way take the right fork, up to the next signpost. Bear right for a few metres along a piece of old walled lane, then turn left to the next signpost, then half right across the field to a ladder-stile. Now walk forward with the remains of a wall on the right to the next signpost** *(there is a* *good view to Stanbury and Lower Laithe Reservoir below it),* **where you fork left to the next ladder-stile. Keep forward onto the moor, soon crossing over two good tracks, at the second of which you are joined by the Pennine Way, to cross a stile into a broad walled lane.**

When the lane ends, keep on by the wall on the right. *There is a splendid view over Ponden Reservoir.* **At the bottom turn right down the track past Buckley Green Farm and immediately hairpin left along another track. Just before the lane becomes tarmac at Buckley Farm, cross the stile on the right and follow the path downhill. On reaching the tarmac lane by Ponden Reservoir dam, the Brontë Way turns left by the reservoir,** but the circular walk turns right down to Ponden Mill, *where refreshments are available (Mon-Sat 9.30-5.30, Sun 11-5).* On reaching the motor road past the mill, cross to the stile opposite and walk along with a wall on the left and the beck on the right.

Ford a side beck and cross a ladder-stile on the left, then bear right along the fence on the right. A few metres before this fence turns sharp right to meet a wall, turn left up the bank on a faint path to a stile in a wall. Bear slightly left up the next field to the next stile (actually two stiles in fences a metre apart), cross over the track and the stile in the wall, and bear half left up the next field to a gateway in the top corner. Continue half left up the next field to a stile by a large metal gate, then half left up the next field to a stile in the top corner, and now follow the wall on your right to Oldfield End Farm.

Go through a gate, cross the farm access drive and go through the gate opposite, to walk straight along the field, with the farm to your right, soon to pick up and follow a wall on the right, which leads to a stile into the next field. Keep along the fence on your right to a step-stile in the next facing wall. Walk forward up the access drive of Wild Fell House. Pass through a gate and keep on up the drive to reach a tarmac lane. Turn left up this to Oldfield Lane. Cross and turn left along the footway, but immediately past Oldfield First School cross the stile on the right and walk up the snicket, a narrow walled lane, to the next road. Turn right to return to the starting point.

Ponden Reservoir to Wycoller
Walk 8

Length of circular walk: 9½ miles (15¼ km). _Length of Brontë Way:_ 4½ miles (7¼ km). _Without doubt the most beautiful section of the Way, up a tranquil valley with lovely old farmhouses, becoming a remote beckside path through bracken, then airy paths and tracks over the Yorkshire-Lancashire watershed, and finally another peaceful valley. The return route is, with one variation, the outward route in reverse, but in view of the quality of the scenery this is no hardship._

Map: Outdoor Leisure 21.

Start and Finish: Ponden Reservoir. Take the access road to Ponden Mill, continue past the car park and on up the minor road to the reservoir. Park along here on the stony verge.

By bus: The M6 is an infrequent service from Keighley to Haworth which passes Ponden Mill. Otherwise you will have to take the No. 22/24/25 (roughly hourly) Keighley-Burnley bus as far as Laneshaw Bridge and walk to Wycoller by the route described at the start of Walk 9, then start the circuit at [*].

PONDEN HALL
STANBURY. NR. HAWORTH

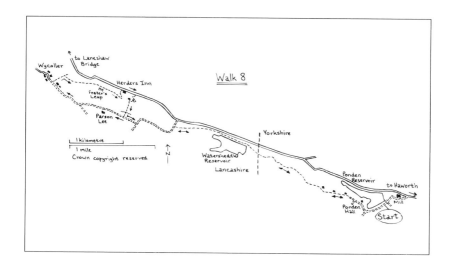

Walk along the road past the reservoir. *The deeply incised valley ahead is Ponden Clough.* **When the road forks, keep right. The road climbs and bends left and Ponden Hall is on the right.** *Built in 1634 and rebuilt in 1807, Ponden Hall was the home of the Heaton family. Emily Brontë borrowed books from their well-stocked library. She used the house as the model for Thrushcross Grange, the home of the Lintons, in her novel 'Wuthering Heights'. Long distance walkers are welcomed here by the owner and her family. Refreshments are available if they are at home.* **At Ponden Hall the tarmac ends: keep forward along the track. Ignore a concrete track forking left uphill and keep forward, once more on tarmac. On reaching a gate across the lane, fork left on a path between fences. Cross a stile ahead into a walled lane** *(the Pennine Way turns right here down another walled lane).* **A few metres before the gate into the garden of the next house bear left to a ladder-stile and walk along the bottom of the field with the house on the right. Keep forward until a waymark post points you right into a walled lane. Follow it as it bends left and in a few metres go through a gateway in the wall on the right.**

Bear slightly right down the next field to the far corner, cross a sleeper bridge and broken wall and walk uphill with a wall on your right. At the top ignore the gate ahead into the yard of a house and bear left, still with the wall on your right to pass through a gateway ahead. Now bear left uphill with a wall on your left. Cross a stile into a walled lane at the end of which cross a ladder-stile by a gate on the right and bear slightly left to follow the clear path towards the valley. Drop to pass through a gap in a wall, and now you have a wall on your right. On approaching the valley bottom, the path bears left away from the wall through the bracken, parallel to the beck down on your right.

Follow the clear path forward until a marker post points you right over a wooden footbridge. The path now bears left and climbs gently. Cross several stiles and pass through several wall-gaps to reach the Yorkshire/Lancashire boundary stone. After another ladder-stile you reach the top of the slope.
Bear left to pass to the left of a barn (the motor road is just over the wall on your right), cross a ladder-stile ahead and walk along by the side of Watersheddles Reservoir.

'JANE EYRE'

The path leads to another ladder-stile. Over this turn left and follow a narrow path with the wall on your left. Having crossed a footbridge, keep on with a fence on the left. Ignore a gate in this fence, but when further on you come to a kissing-gate in it, go through and now follow a very good path, for the first few metres with the fence on the right. On reaching another kissing-gate Pendle Hill comes into view ahead and you reach a cross track. Turn left down this. After quite some distance the track climbs and bends left to reach a footpath signpost. *Here you join the Pendle Way.* **Cross the stile by the gate on the right and walk down the grassy way.**

The path crosses a stile with a curious road sign beside it and passes below Parson Lee Farm to join the farm access road, soon a beautiful tree-lined track with the beck on the right. At the next junction, just before a stone bridge, the continuation of the Brontë Way is the access track to Dean House Farm on the left. But first we shall follow the track forward into the hamlet of Wycoller. *Look out for Clam Bridge over Wycoller Beck, formed by a solid block of gritstone and believed to date from the Iron Age. The next bridge is the stone arched Copy House Bridge, soon followed by the picnic site, toilets*

WYCOLLER HALL
(RUINS)

and Information Centre in the Aisled Barn. Opposite the ruined Wycoller Hall, 16th-century in origin and extended in 1774 by Squire Cunliffe, is an ancient clapper bridge, and a little further on is a double arched packhorse bridge thought to have been built between the 13th and 15th centuries. There are several most attractive houses in the hamlet.

   Wycoller was once a cottage industry hamlet until the Industrial Revolution when it became 'abandoned' as workers moved to homes nearer the mills. Now it is a popular tourist attraction, very busy on summer weekends, but delightfully renovated and preserved. The Hall was said to be the model for Ferndean Manor in Charlotte Brontë's novel 'Jane Eyre'. There is a café which is open in the summer every day except Monday 11-5 and at weekends in the winter. Cars are not encouraged

into the village, but there are *two designated car parks* *nearby. One is signposted off* *the Haworth/Laneshaw Bridge* *road 'Lancashire County* *Council' Haworth Road Car* *Park for Wycoller Country* *Park and the other is on the* *Trawden/Wycoller road a* *kilometre's walk from Wycoller.*

(Walkers who are here finishing the third section of their linear walk and want to get to Laneshaw Bridge for a bus should follow the route description given at the end of this walk.)

[*] Circular walkers could make the entire return to Ponden Reservoir on their outward route, but I suggest a short variation at the start. It involves some quite steep ascent and descent, but the rewards are superb views, Foster's Leap, another local attraction, and the possibility of visiting a charming and friendly pub. If all that appeals to you, then take the cobbled steps up behind the ruined Hall. *At the top notice the wall on the left made from upright stones: there are several of these walls around here, known as vaccary walls, and they are thought to have been built for cattle farms in the 13th century.* Pass between old gateposts and continue up the track, known as the Old Coach Road.

Just before the way ahead splits, cross the stile by the gate on the right and bear slightly left across the field to the stile and gate on the far side. Now follow the fence on the right to a gap in a cross wall, then bear slightly left steeply uphill on a clear path. Pass through the next broken down cross wall and go half left uphill to a wall corner, then bear right with the wall on your right to a ladder-stile. *The views up here are splendid.* Continue with the wall on your right, but when it begins to curve gently right, keep straight forward to reach a tarmac access road. Keep your line diagonally

over this and walk on uphill, passing to the left of a wooden telegraph pole and aiming for the top side of the jumble of rocks.

The narrow space between two of the large rocks is known as Foster's Leap, supposedly from a jump made by Foster Cunliffe, a relative of the Cunliffes of Wycoller Hall. Keep forward on the path above the rocks to reach a wall corner, then continue with the wall on your left. After some time it suddenly drops very sharply. Follow it down - there is an easier route slightly to the right - and at the foot cross the step-stile in the wall and walk back up the slope with the wall on your left! On reaching a cross fence turn right along it to a small wooden gate beside a large metal one. Through this walk forward to pass through another wooden gate and bear right through the car park of the Herders Inn.

This fine old building has been an inn since about 1860. Before that the families who lived there were employed in handloom weaving, but it is said that originally two herder's cottages stood on the site. The interior is charming and the welcome warm, and the pub is open Monday-Friday 11.30-3 and 7-11 and all day on Saturday and Sunday.

Bear right along the road past the inn. After 300 metres, just before a large layby on the right, a footpath sign points right. Walk down the path, which bears right to a stile in the wall on the left. A hollow way now bears left and drops to reach a farm access road. Bear right along this, passing Higher Key Stiles Farm, to a gate into Lower Key Stiles Farm. Go through and on along the track, turning left through a small wooden gate opposite the end of a building on the right. Walk straight down the hill, soon to pick up and follow a wall on the left. When the rushes begin, the ground is very wet, so try to step on the rushes. When the wall turns left, keep straight on down. There's a very steep drop to the beck. Pass through a stile in the wall, ford the beck - there are useful large stones - and walk straight up the other side to reach a track. Turn left along this, and now you are on your outward route. Follow it back to Ponden Reservoir.

(Route from Wycoller village to Laneshaw Bridge for the bus.) Follow the road through the village, turn left over the bridge, then right along a track behind houses. Bear right over another bridge. Keep forward over a stile and through a kissing-gate and follow the wall on your left. Cross a stile in it, ascend a few steps and follow the wall on the right to the next stile. In a few metres pass through a wooden gate and cross a footbridge, then follow the path over the next very large field to another gate. The path is now clear to the next road. Turn right along it, then left at the T-junction, and walk up to the main road and the bus.

Wycoller to Thursden
Walk 9

Length of circular walk: 8¾ miles (14 km). _Length of Brontë Way:_ 5¼ miles (8½ km). A varied pastoral route past some attractive houses and with superb views is followed by a long moorland tramp on a good track. A large part of the route of the Way coincides with the Pendle Way.

Map: Outdoor Leisure 21.

Start and finish: Just off the minor road from Hebden Bridge to Colne at GR 901 351 there is a large layby with a picnic site in the field below it and splendid views over the Thursden valley and down to Burnley. Start here. The walk could also be started from either of the Wycoller Country Park car parks (on Trawden Road or Haworth Road). In that case you would need first to walk into the village, then start the walk at [*] below.

By bus: No. 22/24/25 (roughly hourly) Keighley-Burnley as far as Laneshaw Bridge. Walk to Wycoller by the Pendle Way (well signposted) by going down School Lane, the minor road opposite the Emmott Arms, crossing the bridge and turning right along Carriers Row. At the end of the terrace of cottages and before the next bridge turn left along the signposted footpath, passing through a kissing-gate and continuing along a stony track. At the end of the stony section keep forward along a broad grassy path. Pass through a small gate and follow the path over the next very large field to a footbridge and another wooden gate.

In a few metres cross a stile in the wall/fence on the right and turn left with the wall on your left. Having descended a few steps, pass through a stile ahead and turn right to follow the wall on your right. The paved path leads to a kissing-gate, from which keep forward. After a time a stile gives access to a track which soon crosses Wycoller Beck and bears left behind some houses. At the road turn left, cross the bridge and turn right with the road into Wycoller village. Start the walk at [*] below, and at the end of the walk return to Laneshaw Bridge by the same route.

Turn left out of the car park and walk along the road in the Burnley direction. Opposite the first minor road on the left, Ridehalgh Lane, cross the signposted step-stile in the wall on the right and walk up the right hand edge of the paddock to a stile at the top. Cross it and the next stile in the fence on the right and bear slightly left across the field to the next stile in a broken wall opposite. Now bear half left to the next stile a few metres to the left of a metal gate in the wire fence. Keep the same line over the next

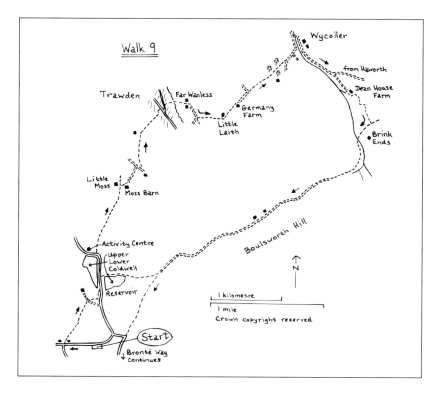

field to the stile in the wall in the top corner. Cross it and walk straight over the next field to the step-stile at the wall corner opposite.

There is a fine view ahead and half left. Can you see Penyghent? Walk down the next field parallel to the wall on the left with the Lower Coldwell Reservoir visible ahead, pass a small pen with a container for pheasant food, and as you approach the bottom of the field bear right to a step-stile in the wall 20 metres to the right of the gate. Cross the farm track diagonally right to the stile opposite and continue with the wall on your left. When the wall ends bear half left and follow the trees along, parallel to the road below, then drop half right to a stile out onto the road and turn left. The road curves left, and with the Outdoor Centre about 150 metres further along the road, turn right through a signposted kissing-gate by a wooden gate and walk straight up the rough pasture, bearing if anything very slightly left.

Coldwell Inn Activity Centre, situated in an 18th-century coaching inn, is a group residential centre for indoor and outdoor activities. Its facilities include an information centre and tearoom (open Monday-Friday 10.30-3, Saturday/Sunday 11-4).

51

As you cross the brow of the slope, you will see that you are heading for a wooden ladder-stile (actually the left hand of two stiles a considerable distance apart) in the wall at the top of the field. Walk half right across the corner of the next field to a gate in the fence, then continue your line across the next large field, passing round a pit used as a tip, and as you progress, you will see that you are heading down to a stile in a wall at the bottom of the field, with a plantation of trees beyond. Our next goal is the top right hand corner of this plantation. At first there is no clear path, so walk boldly forward through the tall grass, and in a few metres a faint path develops, which soon leads to a clear grassy path which takes you up to a gateway in the top corner.

Keep forward with the wall on your right, pass through a large metal gate straight ahead in the next corner, ignoring the gate on the right, and keep the wall still on your right. A short distance along, before you reach Little Moss Farm, cross the step-stile in the wall and bear half left down the field to a small gate just in front of the next house, Moss Barn. Go through and pass to the left of the house, then bear left through a gateway and down the access track. *Is it clear enough for you to see Ingleborough?* On reaching a cross track turn right for 40 metres, then go left through a stile 5 metres before a power line pole and walk down the edge of the field with the wall on your left.

Cross the stile in the next corner, Trawden is now ahead, and continue with the wall/fence on your left. When the wall turns sharp left by a power line pole, go slightly left to a stile on the far side of the field, but instead of going through it, turn down the edge of the field with the wall on your left. Go through the gate in the next field corner and continue down with the wall on your left. In the corner of this field go through a gated stile and walk down an enclosed path, turn left along a tarmac path to reach a street, then turn right for a few metres to a signposted tarmac footpath on the right, which leads down to a road. The centre of Trawden is to the left, but we cross the road, bear right past the bus shelter and turn left down a cobbled lane with iron rails embedded in it.

In 30 metres look out for a stile on the right just past a double wooden gate. The path leads down to a stile into a field: walk straight over to cross Trawden Brook by a footbridge, cross the stile beyond and bear right up through the trees parallel to a wall on the left. At the top of the steep slope follow the path forward to Far Wanless Farm, and on reaching a wall corner keep forward to enter the farm precincts through an iron gate. Pass between the buildings and walk forward up a track (look back to admire this lovely 17th-century farmhouse), bearing right to pass through a stile by a metal gate. Continue along the track parallel to a wall on the right. Pass through an old gateway, and the track acquires a fence on the left. When the track curves right to a cattle-grid, ignore the stile straight ahead and turn left through the gated stile and follow the right hand edge of the field up.

Pass to the left of a small shelter belt and continue up the field edge to a stile in the top corner. Cross this and keep forward with the wall on your right to Little Laith Farm. Pass the cattle-grid and go through the second small gate on the right (the one beside the large gate), then turn left along the bottom of the field with the farm and a wall on the left. Cross the next stile just in front of Germany Farm and bear left round the farmhouse to join a track on the far side. Follow this until the main track turns left, when you keep forward along a minor track, but when this goes through a gate on the right, keep straight on with the fence to your right. Cross a stile and little bridge and keep following the fence.

Cross another bridge and a rather splendid stone stile in the field corner, and now you have a wall on your right. Go through a kissing-gate and straight across the next field, keeping left of a short piece of wall jutting into it at the far side, to where a small wooden gate is followed by another very fine stone stile, and now walk down through

the wood to a kissing-gate at the bottom, down the stepped path to a track, and bear left down the track. At the foot of the hill, with Wycoller Beck ahead, follow the track left for the centre of the village or cross the clapper bridge to the ruined Hall and turn right for the Information Centre, toilets, picnic area and pond.

[*] To continue the Brontë Way from Wycoller, return along the track by which you arrived on the previous walk, with Wycoller Beck on your right, but when the track splits keep right, taking the access track to Dean House Farm. Enter the yard of the farm and bear left to pass in front of the house, keep forward to a stile

beside the metal gate ahead, then keep forward along the track, in 25 metres crossing another stile by a large metal gate, and continue up the track with a wall on the right. It is easy to go astray on the next section, so please follow the directions carefully. When the wall turns sharp right, the track turns half right, but almost immediately fork left off it, pass round to the right of a deep hollow in the ground and walk up to the end of a wall above, then keeping this wall and then a fence on your right, walk up to a ladder-stile in the next facing wall just to the left of a gate.

Bear slightly right towards the next wall and turn right along the clear path a metre or two before it. You have now joined the Pendle Way, and now route finding becomes very easy. Brink Ends Farm is high above on the left. Follow the path down to a double wooden gate, go through and descend into Turnhole Clough. Ford the beck and follow the track as it winds up the other side. You follow this clear path/track for the next 3¾ kilometres, usually with a wall on the right and with the slopes of Boulsworth Hill up on the left. Intermittent paving shows that this is an old route. For a time the track acquires a tarmac surface. *Watch out for good views over the wall, for example over Trawden to Ingleborough.*

A good way along, coming over the brow of a hill, Upper and Lower Coldwell Reservoirs become visible and there is a good view of Pendle Hill further off. Shortly after this, at a marker post, we part company with the Pendle Way, which keeps forward along the better path, while the Brontë Way forks left along a narrow trod through tussocky grass. Be careful not to miss this junction! There is one stile to cross along this path, and shortly after it you cross a wooden footbridge and climb a little slope. At the top there is a marker post: ignore the arrow pointing right, and keep forward along the clearer path, which soon passes to the right of the stone gable end of New House Farm which has two inscribed stones in it, both dated 1672.

The path continues through the thick grass. Cross a stile by a gate and keep forward over the next field to the next stile by the next gate, then bear right with the track to the road. **The Brontë Way turns left down the road,** but to return to the car bear right up the road and follow it to the next road junction, there turning left and passing an old pill-box in the field on the right.

Thursden to Netherwood Bridge
Walk 10

Length of circular walk: 7 miles (11¼ km). _Length of Brontë Way:_ 3¾ miles (6 km). Two delightful valleys and more fine views. The route coincides in a number of places with the Burnley Way.

Map: Outdoor Leisure 21.

Start and finish: As in walk 9. A good deal of the walk can actually be seen from this point.

By bus: 9/10/11 Burnley-Nelson-Blacko, 78 Burnley-Harle Syke-Nelson to Netherwood Road, Heasandford. Walk along Netherwood Road for 1 km, until just after passing a Lancashire County Council car park on the left you reach Netherwood Bridge. Cross and continue on the track to Netherwood Farm, joining the walk description at [*].

From the layby walk along the road with the Thursden valley down on your right. Just before you reach the next road junction, notice the old concrete pill-box on the left. Fork right at the junction (signposted Hebden Bridge). Just before the road bends right ignore a footpath sign on the right. Follow the road round the bend. The Brontë Way joins it through a gate on the left.

Walk down the road for about 60 metres, where there is a public footpath sign on the right. Ignore the stile in the fence on the right and continue along the road for a further 10 metres to find a flight of steps on the right leading down into the wood. The Way is marked by faded yellow stripes on the trees. A reasonably clear path descends through the wood and leaves it by a stile at the bottom. Turn left down a fenced track, crossing a bridge and going through a gate to reach a metalled road in the Thursden valley. Turn right along the road but just before it begins to climb cross a stile on the left and follow a pleasant winding path between stream and a wall. Cross a footbridge and climb uphill through the wood to a fence stile.

Having crossed the stile, you will see two paths on the left. The right fork is the Burnley Way, the left one, climbing to the right of a wall, is the Brontë Way. When the wall/fence on the left turns sharp left, bear half right to follow another wall on your left. In 30 metres pass through a wide gap in this wall and continue up with

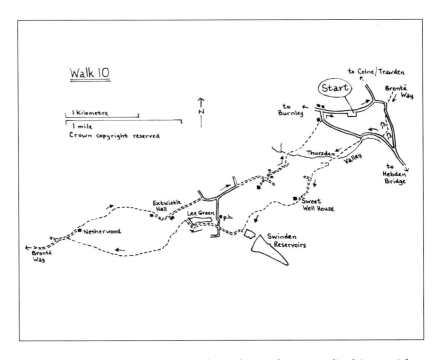

the wall now on your right. **When the path stops climbing, with a fine view to Pendle Hill and Burnley, a finger-post points left and the path climbs up the field to a ladder-stile in the wall at the top by a small rowan tree. Keep forward up the tarmac farm access road to Sweet Well House Farm. Enter the farmyard and keep along the wall on your left to a stone step stile in it and walk down the field curving right with a wall on your right, descending into a valley.**

Soon you are on a good track which leads to a ladder-stile. Keep forward down the clear path with the wall always on your right, at one point ignoring a ladder-stile in it. Cross a ladder-stile by a gate near the corner of one of the Swinden Reservoirs and continue down the track for a few metres to a step-stile by another gate leading out onto a tarmac lane. Keep forward along this to the main road at Swinden Bridge. *(If refreshment is needed here, turn right and a five minutes walk up the hill is Roggerbamgate Inn. No accommodation is offered but food and drinks are available. To continue walking on the Brontë Way, retrace steps down the hill and turn right into the double-walled grassy lane.)*

Cross straight over the road into the walled lane opposite, passing through a kissing gate. Walk round two sides of Lee Green Reservoir and pass two interestingly shaped buildings within the waterworks grounds to a stone step stile. *(Looking half left up the slope the tall old building is Extwistle Hall, which we shall pass later on the return walk.)* Turn left on a clear path, soon being joined once more by the Burnley Way. Now follows a delightful walk down the valley of Swinden Water. After a time the path is intermittently paved. At times it is near the beck, at times some way above it. At one point two stiles close together lead over a side beck, and then the path leads through woodland. Look out for a fork, where you keep right (fingerpost). Shortly after you cross a stile a sleeper bridge leads over another side beck.

Soon you are following the remains of an old hedge on the right. Look out for a fingerpost, where you must turn sharp left down into the valley again, then sharp right at the bottom of the slope. Soon the beck is again close by on the left. The path leads across a large grassy area, passing a fingerpost. Cross another stile back into woodland and immediately the path forks. Keep right. Descend some steps, cross a footbridge over a side beck, and climb some steps on the other side to follow a fence on the right. Descend some more steps with the beck close by on the left. Pass a well-built footbridge to reach the confluence of the Swinden Water and the River Brun, which gives its name to Burnley. Pass a wooden barrier onto a track.

Brontë Way walkers will turn left and cross Netherwood Bridge, where the River Don joins the Brun. The Burnley Way goes off through a barrier on the right, the Brontë Way continues forward along the wide track, shortly reaching a car park which will be the start of the next walk for circular walkers. Those wishing to return to the start of the present circular walk will, having passed the wooden barrier, turn right up the track.

[*] Walk straight through the farmyard at Netherwood, cross the stile by the gate at the far end and continue forward along the track, soon with a hedge/fence on the right. Cross three stiles beside gates, keeping always the fence on the right. *You have now rejoined the Burnley Way.* The fourth stile by a gate is between the fence on the right and a wall on the left, and now you are following a wall on the left. Cross the stile

by the next gate and keep on by the wall to Houghton's Farm, where you cross another stile by a gate and walk through the yard. At the far end continue along the track with a wall on the right. Cross a cattle grid and follow the track past Extwistle Hall, a fine 17th-century house now sadly derelict.

Down below on the right is Lee Green Reservoir, and the Burnley Way crosses a stile on the right to descend to it. Our route lies on along the track to the next road, then on up the road. Where the main road turns sharp right, keep forward up the minor road signposted Shay Lane. *As you climb this road you can see the picnic site you are heading for in the distance.* Ignore a tarmac lane forking left. Where the access road to Elders i' th' Row Farm forks off right, turn left off the tarmac road (there is a cattle grid ahead) into a stony track which leads past kennels on the right and through the buildings of Monk Hall. It is tarmac for a short length, then unsurfaced between walls.

Cross a stile by a gate across the track, and when in a few metres the wall on the left turns left downhill, go with it, *here joining yet again the Burnley Way.* Cross a stile by a gate and keep forward, to find yourself on the edge of a precipitous drop into the valley of Thursden Brook. Fortunately there are steps leading down, but this is a spectacular descent. Cross the beck by the footbridge, climb a few steps and follow the fence on the right to a stile in a few metres. Cross it and turn left uphill over rough ground, parallel to the fence/wall on the left but gradually drawing closer to it. Ignore a stile in it *(here we finally part company with the Burnley Way)* and follow the wall on the left up. Cross a stile by a gate and now follow the fence on the right.

Cross the stile in the fence ahead and walk straight up the next field to a stile to the right of a gate. Keep forward up the track, but when you reach the lawn, bear right with the track to join the tarmac access drive, which you follow up to the road (this is not the route of the right of way, but it is more convenient and is used by permission of the house owners). Turn left here, then at the T-junction right, to return to your starting point.

Netherwood Bridge to Gawthorpe Hall
Walk 11

Length of circular walk: 12 miles (19¼ km). *Length of Brontë Way:* 6¼ miles (10¼ km). Very easy walking, much of it by canal and river.

Map: Outdoor Leisure 21.

Start and finish: Car park on Netherwood Road, Heasandford, Burnley. Netherwood Road leaves the A6114 just north of where this road crosses the River Brun at Heasandford. Drive along this lane, the surface of which leaves much to be desired, keep right at a fork, until having passed a large factory the road narrows and the car park is some way further along on the left.

By public transport: 9/10/11 Burnley-Nelson-Blacko, 78 Burnley-Harle Syke-Nelson to Netherwood Road, Heasandford. Walk along Netherwood Road for 1 km to a Lancashire County Council car park on the left.

'THE SHUTTLEWORTHS'

Leave the car park and turn right along the track. **Where the road bends right at the end of the factory buildings, the Brontë Way continues straight on by a path between the river Brun on the left and allotments on the right,** *being joined yet again by the Burnley Way.* **Go under the road bridge and walk through Bank Hall Park alongside the river, then under an arched bridge which carries the Leeds and Liverpool canal.**

In 25 metres turn right up some steps and follow the path to the canal towpath, where you turn left for a good half hour's walk under a series of bridges, the first of which is a stone arch. At the second green iron road bridge Pendle Hill can be seen in the distance ahead. The third is a rusty footbridge. The fourth another stone arch bridge. The fifth a railway bridge. The sixth another footbridge. The seventh is a road bridge and at the eighth bridge turn left to where a Brontë Way sign in the dip points into a field over a wooden stile. Bear half right over the field to a stile in a fence, then continue downhill, bearing slightly left to pick up a good path bearing left with trees and Pendle Water on the right. *Here you are joined by the Pendle Way.* **The path leads to a kissing-gate and a road.**

Turn right over New in Pendle Bridge, turn left immediately along Wood End, then right up a track past Pendle Bridge cottages to a

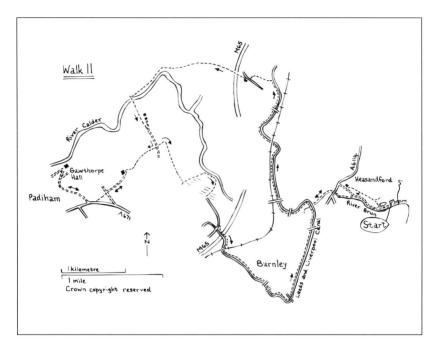

stile. Bear right round the edge of the field and follow it to a stile in the top corner. Cross this and the next one on the left, and cross the M65 motorway by a footbridge. Turn right down to a stile by a signpost, then turn left up the left hand edge of the field. In a short distance look out for a wooden bridge on the left which is well hidden in the bushes. After crossing the bridge turn right along the edge of the field, cross three stiles on the way, then keep forward, soon dropping to the right of a large ash tree, to cross a wooden footbridge and the stile beyond. Keep forward up the bank, pass a signpost, cross a tarmac farm road and keep forward over the next very large field, aiming well to the left of a large pylon.

In a dip, well before you reach the pylon, cross a wooden bridge, after which the path forward is clear. It crosses a sleeper bridge. Cross a side beck (the stile beyond is redundant) and bear slightly left to reach the bank of the River Calder. Very soon you cross another side beck by a substantial footbridge. Cross another stile, and the path is parallel to the river. Keep forward over level pasture, but when you see a track forking right up the bank, walk to the start of it, but then follow a path along the foot of the bank. This avoids wet places in the field which can be awkward. The path

climbs slightly to reach the end of the bridge, by which you cross the river, *here losing the Pendle Way but rejoining the Burnley Way.*

From the bridge walk forward to a stile and bear right along a clear grassy path which climbs uphill away from the river, passing well to the right of a large barn, eventually with a hedge/fence on the left. Cross the stile into a tarmac lane and follow it up to a house on the right called Clynders Cottage. *Here there is a stile on the left, which will be used on our return route,* **but the Way continues by turning right just past the houses along a ginnel signposted Habergham 1 mile. Cross a stile and keep forward along the left hand edge of the field. There is one very wet patch on the way.** *There is a pleasant view right over the Calder valley and to Pendle Hill.* **Cross another stile and continue by the field edge, soon joining a track.** *The trees in Gawthorpe Hall grounds can be seen ahead but the Hall itself is hidden.*

Cross two more stiles and follow the track to the farm. Turn left in front of the large barn, pass through a gate and a few metres further on cross a stile by a gate on the right and walk through the farmyard, then cross a stile by a gate on the left and follow the farm access road. Cross over a tarmac lane and follow the path opposite down to the A671. Turn right and take the second access road on the right to enter the grounds of Gawthorpe Hall at the lodge gates.

The Shuttleworth family have been connected with Gawthorpe and the estate since the 14th century. They were strongly associated with weaving in both wool and cotton. In Charlotte Brontë's generation the Shuttleworths were local philanthropists with emphasis on 'education for the workpeople' and no doubt on her visits to the Hall education would be a talking point. Charlotte became a good friend of Lady Kay Shuttleworth who introduced her to Mrs Gaskell whilst they were in Windermere in the summer of 1850.

Shortly after passing a fine wrought iron gate, you meet a rather better track on a bend. Keep left down this to the Hall and the end of the Brontë Way.

Gawthorpe Hall, built in 1600-5 and restored by Sir Charles Barry in the 1850s is now owned by the National Trust. It is open from Easter to the end of October daily except Monday and Friday from 1-5. There is a tearoom open the same days as the Hall, 12.30-4.30.

GAWTHORPE HALL

Circular walkers will now retrace their steps to Clynders Cottage. Cross the stile by the gate opposite and walk along the field edge with a wood on the right. When the edge of the wood turns right, go with it, here once more joining the Burnley Way, which we shall follow almost all the way back to the start. Cross the stile in the next corner and keep forward across the top side of the next field to the stile by the gate ahead. Cross the track and the stile opposite and walk over the next field to the stile in the far corner. This is clearly a very 'horsey' area! Keep along the right hand edge of the next field, cross a stile to the left of a gate ahead in the next corner and continue forward across the next large field. Near the far side you pass through an old hedge, and ahead is a stile with a high wooden fence and modern houses beyond.

Turn left down the enclosed path. Pass the redundant stile at the bottom and keep forward to the left of a new housing development. Soon the path is again enclosed. It drops to the river. Bear right parallel to the river, soon joining a track along the left hand edge of a field. Follow the track as it turns right up to some more houses, cross the stile and keep forward with a high fence on the left. Turn left along the first street and follow it for quite some way until you reach a bridge over the Leeds and Liverpool Canal. Immediately before this bridge fork left down onto the towpath and bear left along it, in a few metres crossing the M65.

Follow the towpath through the centre of Burnley. The most picturesque spot is Burnley Wharf, with the old canal toll house, inn and Weavers Triangle Visitor Centre. When you pass a large park on the left, with boating lake, children's playground and paddling pool, with the Queen Victoria pub on the other side of the canal, your towpath walk is almost over. Immediately after the canal crosses the River Brun fork left down the path you came up earlier and turn left at the foot of the steps. Retrace your route until you reach the road with the large factory opposite. Here you could keep forward along the road to return to the car park, but if you would like to keep following the Burnley Way for a short distance further, turn left along the road.

The road passes the rather elegant Heasandford Villa and curves left. A short way along follow a footpath signpost pointing right along a path into woodland. Follow the fence on the right, keeping right at the next footpath junction. At the next junction, where the Burnley Way turns left on the better path uphill, keep straight on along a narrower path, soon reaching a lake. Follow the path by the lake to the far end, where a stile gives access to the car park.

DID YOU KNOW that you can walk out of Leeds City Station, turn right and in a few minutes find yourself on a direct footpath route to the source of the River Aire, 50 miles away at Malham Tarn in the heart of the Yorkshire Dales?

Details of the whole route, which follows as far as possible riverside paths, are given in Douglas Cossar's *The Airedale Way*.

The book contains 16 circular and 2 linear rambles which cover the whole of Airedale from Malham Tarn to Castleford and include the entire towpath of the Leeds and Liverpool Canal between Leeds and Gargrave. Riverside paths and walks to notable viewpoints open up a variety of landscapes and a wealth of natural beauty, with old stone bridges, ancient churches, picturesque villages, historic farmhouses and many relics of the Industrial Revolution.

The Airedale Way is published by the West Riding Area of the RA at **£4.50** and is available from local booksellers, or direct from the publishers at 27 Cookridge Avenue, Leeds LS16 7NA price £5.50 including post & packing (cheques payable to Ramblers' Association please).

ACCOMMODATION

There are no Youth Hostels near Oakwell Hall, but bed and breakfast may be booked in advance at The White Bear, High Street, Birstall, West Yorkshire (01924-476212). Also Oakwell Motel, Low Lane, Birstall (01924-441514).

There are a few bed and breakfast/guest houses in Hartshead. To make a reservation contact Kirklees Tourist Information Centre, 3-5 Albion Street, Huddersfield HD1 2NW (01484-430808).

There is no listed overnight accommodation in Bailiff Bridge. The nearest suggested bed and breakfast is in Brighouse. Contact Calderdale Tourist Information Centre, Piece Hall, Halifax, West Yorkshire HX1 1RE (01422-368725).

If accommodation is required in the Bradford area enquiries can be made at the Tourist Information Centre which is in the Central Library, Princes Way, Bradford BD1 1NN (01274-753678). During your stay, a visit to a curry house is a must!

Accommodation in Haworth is plentiful and too numerous to mention all individually. Contact the Haworth Tourist Information Centre 2/4 West Lane, Haworth BD22 8EF (01535-642329, FAX 01535-647721) for current list and prices. Haworth Youth Hostel, Longlands Drive, Lees Lane, Haworth BD22 8RT (01535-642234) is one and a half kilometres from Haworth village centre along the B6142 road to Keighley.

Accommodation and evening meal at Ponden Hall, Stanbury, near Haworth, West Yorkshire (01535-644154) must be booked in advance by telephone and confirmed with a deposit. Rates are £17 per person bed and breakfast. Evening meal £9. The food is plentiful, fresh and home-cooked in an original manner. Well recommended. Free car parking at the side of the tarmac on an unmade road on the edge of the reservoir.

One kilometre before Wycoller village is a peaceful farmhouse offering accommodation. A warm welcome awaits you from Mrs Pat Hodgson, Parson Lee Farm, Wycoller, Colne BB8 8SU (01282-864747). Pre-booking is advisable. Accommodation is also available from Mrs Margaret Houlker, Wycoller Cottage, Wycoller, Colne BB8 8SY (01282-867336), a 17th century listed building of character overlooking the ruins of Wycoller Hall. Two rooms, one ensuite.

Accommodation in Padiham. Mr and Mrs Williams, Trevelyn Guest House, 28 Church Street, Padiham BB12 8HG (01282-771804). A friendly welcome awaits you at this family run guest house near to Padiham town centre. 8 ensuite rooms.

Windsor House, Mrs Stinton, 71 Church Street, Padiham BB12 8JH (01282-773231). Homely accommodation in Padiham Conservation Area. 7 rooms.

Crossways, Whalley Road, Padiham, Nr. Burnley BB12 8JR (01282-772423). Elegant Victorian residence converted into a luxury hotel.